EXPLORING THE BACKCOUNTRY OF ZION NATIONAL PARK:

OFF-TRAIL ROUTES

by Thomas Brereton and James Dunaway

Revised and updated, 1996

Zion Natural History Association

© 1996 Published by Zion Natural History Association
Springdale, Utah 84767

Publisher—Jamie Gentry
Edited by Jane Freeburg
Designed by Lucy Brown
Map Graphics by Emmerson & Associates, St. George, Utah
Printed by Paragon Press, Salt Lake City, Utah

Photo Credits
All photography courtesy of Zion National Park.
Tom Bereton: Cover, 1, 9, 39, 40, 42 top, 43, 44
James Dunaway: 15, 31, 33, 34, 41, 55, 82, 83
Alan Hagood: 37
Victor L. Jackson: 6, 13, 42, 45, 49 bottom
National Park Service: 36, 38, 59, 65, 89

ISBN 0-915630-25-7

Important Hiker Information

Users are responsible for their own safety and survival.

What is an **off-trail route?** It is *not a trail* and usually not a path; in certain places you can't even stand up. In some spots you must climb, crawl, use a rope or swim. An off-trail route is an unmarked cross-country "way" that takes the hiker somewhere, often involving considerable personal effort, and requiring knowledge of one's capabilities and limitations.

Some of the hikes described in this book are technical in nature. While there are a few that most hikers can make, many are difficult and ambitious undertakings. They lead the visitor into remote backcountry areas where timely *rescue* is unlikely. Please read the route descriptions before beginning a trip so that you know what you are getting into. Wilderness can be unforgiving.

Conditions change in the backcountry. Park rangers make irregular patrols into these areas and may not be informed of changes or dangerous conditions. Terrain features and obstacles may be modified seasonally and appear much different from the written description. You may need additional skills or equipment to complete a hike when conditions are more rigorous. *Inclement weather* can make any of these hikes hazardous.

This book is offered as an aid to experienced off-trail hikers at his or her own risk. It is published and owned by the Zion Natural History Association, and may be updated as necessary in future printings. Give your comments or suggestions to the National Park Service or Zion Natural History Association.

These hikes take you into amazing country. Hike carefully, joyfully, and lightly!

Bob Lineback
Former Backcountry Ranger
Zion National Park

This 1996 Printing was edited for accuracy by NPS Interpretive staff and ZNHA staff, Vauna Lewis and Betsy Alford.

Access: Ingress or egress to some of the routes in Zion National Park involves crossing private land. Access information in this book was correct at time of publication. Please check at a visitor center regarding latest access information before crossing private property.

CONTENTS

HIKING WITH MINIMUM IMPACT

Zion National Park is an extraordinary resource offering the hiker a diversity of experiences. The 147,000-acre (59,500 hectares) park, with elevations ranging from 3,640 to 8,726 feet (1,109 to 2,660 m) supports a wide assortment of plant and animal life in a rich environment of brilliantly-hued canyons, isolated mesas, and etched terraces of slickrock.

The spectrum of wilderness experience

Your hiking trip in Zion National Park will be most enjoyable if you *plan* to make it a safe one. Let a friend or relative know your trip plan and expected return time so they can inform park rangers if you do not return. **Rescue is not a sure or immediate service: be prepared to survive on your own.**

Enjoy the beauty and freedom of Zion's backcountry. With this freedom comes the responsibility to take care of the land, and to leave without signs of your passing. This also reduces the need for additional regulations. Minimum impact principles are an investment in the future integrity of the wilderness. Be it tomorrow or in years to come, let those that follow you have the opportunity to experience a natural Zion National Park.

Appreciate the Sensitivity of the World Around You: Allowing Survival

Zion is a land where only small isolated areas—the mesa tops and sheltered side canyons—seem to escape nature's harsh influence. Vegetation that can survive the extremes in temperatures and soil moisture here can be described as "hardy"—but once disturbed, restoration can be a matter of decades.

Above the narrow canyon creek beds are *sandy benches* formed by water and wind deposited soils. The plants that hold these structures in fragile stability are easily disturbed by foot traffic. Slumping can occur with slight disturbance—rutting develops with repeated use. Hike in the flood plain when possible. If you must cross a bench, tread on lesser slopes and pre-existing paths; avoid stepping on vegetation.

In some areas of the park, particularly in the pinyon-juniper woodland, a community association of lichen and moss grows on the soil, forming a dark, spongy surface called *microbiotic crust.* These fragile areas resist erosion, absorb moisture, and offer favorable sites for the sprouting of plants. Stay on trails, rock, or barren ground where possible—take special care to avoid these fragile soils.

Small, isolated plant communities, called *hanging gardens,* grow at seeps on the canyon walls. Throughout the summer, the delicate green fronds of the ferns are a backdrop to the blossoms of monkey flower, shooting star, columbine, and cardinal flower. These unique habitat areas provide a home to the *Zion snail*—found nowhere else in the world. As with all things in the park, please look and enjoy, but do not touch or disturb.

The Minimum Impact Ethic: Think About What You do

Backcountry travel in Zion does make an impact on this vulnerable, sensitive environment. In everything you do—whether choosing a route, selecting a campsite, or enjoying your camp—there is potential longterm influence.

Stay on trails where they are available; do not shortcut. Avoid or tread lightly in unique and sensitive ecosystems. The survival or destruction of these resources hinges more on your attitude and action than on any list of regulations.

Campsite Selection

Permits are required for all overnight trips and through-trips into the Zion Narrows or its tributaries. "No Camping" areas are posted on visitor center maps; these are generally near roads, trailheads, day use areas, springs, and park inholdings. Always camp away from and out of sight of trails. Camp at least 1/4 mile (.4 km) from any water source (although in narrow canyons this may be impossible). Camping away from springs spreads impact and allows wildlife to drink unhindered by your presence. Avoid making campsite improvements or disturbing even dead vegetation. Do not construct benches, tables, rock or log shelters, or bough beds. If you find items like these, please dismantle and scatter the items so the area looks natural again.

In *desert areas,* choose previously-used campsites or areas of bare soil to localize impact. In *plateau areas,* where ecosystems are more tolerant of use and frost heaving helps eliminate soil compaction, select a campsite that has not been recently occupied, thus spreading out use and allowing natural recovery. In *narrow canyon areas* select a safe site above the high water mark. Go lightly on the benches to prevent hard-to-erase impacts. Avoid vegetation and unstable soils, and direct your activities to sandbars along the river when it is safe.

No open fires are allowed in the Zion backcountry. Campfire impacts are unacceptable—scarring, soil sterilization, loss of humus source materials, and vegetation damage from firewood gathering. Carry a backpacking stove, or plan simple, lightweight "no cook" meals as experienced desert hikers do.

If you carry it in, carry it out. Leave nothing behind or buried, not even food scraps or grease. Help remove litter that other hikers may have dropped. Leave the backcountry wilder and cleaner than when you entered.

Although you may never intentionally feed wildlife, many backcountry campers contribute to wildlife problems by failing to secure their food while they sleep. Skunks, ringtail cats, squirrels, pack rats, and other rodents have been known to chew through nylon materials or expensive backpacks. When you make camp for the night, assume these animals live in the vicinity. If you leave equipment items with food smells on the ground, these small animals will probably get into them. To avoid this, look around your camp carefully and suspend your pack or food sack a few feet off the ground by hanging it with a short cord from a tree branch or stick.

Avoiding Other Impacts

Pets are not allowed away from the roadways or in the backcountry. No matter how well behaved or harmless, pets are a disruption to wildlife patterns and other visitors. Pet kennel services are available in Rockville, Hurricane, St. George, and Cedar City.

Human waste must be buried 1/4 mile (.4 km) from water sources, trails or campsites. Dig a hole 6 to 8 inches (15-20 cm) deep, choosing a spot with dark, rich soil which assists decomposition. Carry out toilet paper—a zip-type plastic bag is a good trash carrier. Leave as little evidence of the hole as you can.

Water should be boiled, treated or filtered before drinking. Surface waters may be contaminated with giardia, a protozoan, or bacteria that can cause serious illness and intestinal problems. Carry water at least 1/4 mile (.4 km) away from the water source to wash dishes, clothes or yourself—using biodegradable soap.

Groups **in the backcountry shall not exceed 12 people in the same drainage, route, or trail on the same day.** This is strictly enforced. Large groups cause greater environmental impacts and diminish the experience of others.

Bicycles and other vehicles are not allowed off the roadways in Zion. Even the tracks of mountain bikes leave unacceptable imprints on the soil. Wilderness is a place where man's machines are intentionally left behind to maintain the primitive experience. In 1995, the park opened a new pedestrian and bicycle trail called the Pa'rus Trail. This trail begins at the southern end of the South Campground and proceeds about 2 miles north to the beginning of the Zion Canyon Scenic Drive. In the future, when the shuttle system is in place in Zion Canyon, the Pa'rus trail will provide access to the Temple of Sinawava free of competition from private autos.

Firearms, electric generators, and chainsaws are not allowed in the backcountry at any time. Thoughtful backcountry hikers do not go down the trail yelling and screaming. Many people enjoy the quiet of the backcountry. Wildlife viewing opportunities increase in the absence of man-made noise.

Zion's sandy soils are ideal for stately Yucca

Taking Care of Yourself:
Recognizing Hazards and Minimizing Risks

Can one enjoy the wilderness without being consumed by its rigors? The key to safe backcountry travel is to take the time to recognize the hazard, calculate the risk, and control the threat. Think!

Physical *fitness* increases your chance of a safe backcountry trip. Traveling in an unfit or overextended condition increases the chances of having an accident. Plan for the severity of the terrain, take your time, and adjust the pace to the slowest member of your group.

Take the proper *equipment,* a good map, and adequate amounts of food and water. When selecting equipment, take only what is necessary and choose the lightest alternative. In summer, wear light-colored clothing, a hat, and sunscreen. In cooler seasons, prepare for rain and snow. Carry enough food and water to last beyond your planned return in case of delays. *Always carry first aid supplies.*

Desert Travel: During summer, when traveling between unknown water sources, carry at least one gallon (4 liters) of water per person per day—and drink it. Heed your body's message when you are thirsty. When you sweat a lot, you should increase your electrolyte intake by drinking fruit juice or including extra salts and sugars in your diet. Be aware of the signs and first aid treatment for heat cramps and heat exhaustion.

Plateau Areas: Anticipate cooler temperatures and possibly rain (snow in the spring or fall). During thunderstorms, minimize lightning danger by avoiding exposed canyon rims and high points. Do not take shelter under lone trees.

Canyon Hikes: Zion's narrow canyons are subject to sudden, unexpected flash flooding. Hiking in these areas requires additional information. *The Zion Narrows Hike (pages 16–23) provides basic reference information useful for hiking any narrow canyon in the Zion area.*

Horses: Zion has minor horse use compared to other western national parks. If you happen to meet some horses along the trail, give them the right of way. Get off the trail and stand quietly while the stock passes. Don't let things blow or flap on your pack, startling the animals.

Fishing: Because of regular sediment flushing during flash floods, fishing is generally poor in the streams and creeks found in Zion. A Utah Fishing License is required if you want to fish in the park.

Other Tips: Keep back from cliff edges. They can be unstable or slippery. Don't roll or throw rocks—this accelerates erosion and destroys vegetation. People may also be hurt below you. Wade or swim only where it is safe; watch out for submerged objects or tricky river currents.

Rattlesnakes: Rattlesnakes are relatively rare. You can avoid them by paying attention to what's on the ground wherever you walk in the park. If climbing or scrambling, check before placing your hand on ledges or in places where reptiles could be.

Zion Seasons: Spring and fall's moderate temperatures are pleasant times for hiking in Zion. In spring, snow run-off will eliminate narrow canyon hiking. In winter, snow and ice conditions close many of Zion's higher elevation backcountry trails, but some lower areas may be accessible. Summer high temperatures in Zion Canyon usually fluctuate around 100°F (38° C). If thunderstorms are absent, summer is a good time for hiking the narrow, shaded canyons. The higher plateaus may also be pleasant when it is hot at the lower elevations.

Insects: Almost all locations in Zion have periods when certain insects can be pesty. Deerflies can be common along creeks in early summer and seem attracted to legs—the best defense is to wear long pants. If it's hot, try wearing pants wet to make hiking cooler.

Tiny gnats called "no-see-ums" can be particularly irritating in late spring and early summer in certain areas. The worst outbreaks last about two weeks at any elevation, with the dates varying from season to season. "No-see-ums" fly about the face and bite the delicate skin around the eyes, neck, or behind the ears. Some people are more sensitive than others to these insects. Various commercial lotions work effectively against "no-see-ums."

Mosquitoes can be bothersome at night in several areas of the park during the summer months. The best defense is a tent with a tight screen door or repellent.

Shuttle Service: Contact the Zion Lodge Transportation Desk or call 801-772-3213 for information on commercial shuttle service to trailheads or starting points.

Publications and Hiker Information

Backcountry permits, topographic maps, publications on hiking trails and backcountry routes, and general interest publications are available at the Zion Canyon and Kolob Canyons Visitor Centers. The National Park Service provides free handouts on pack use, rock climbing, the Narrows, backcountry trails, and the hiker shuttle.

Management: How you can help

Zion National Park is a natural area, thus focusing management on the preservation of biologic and physical features found in this area. Zion gets over 2 million visitors per year. The National Park Service manages the backcountry of Zion with two basic goals: to protect and preserve park resources so that they are available for future generations; and to assure visitors the opportunity for a quality experience. Zion National Park is developing a backcountry management plan to outline policies and procedures that park management will use to implement identified objectives. The plan will be a public document; a statement of long-range management goals. It will also provide strategy and working guidelines for the park staff to use in daily operations.

What can you do to help preserve Zion?

Report any adverse impacts or activities destructive to your park that you see during your trip. Remembering details will help the Park Service investigate the problem. If you see cattle or other livestock on NPS land, please report it.

Lightning-caused *fires* occur during the summer on the plateaus of Zion. Under certain conditions they are beneficial to the ecosystem and are allowed to burn. During fire danger periods most fires are discovered by surveillance from the fire lookout or from observation planes. If you witness a wildfire that is not being monitored, please report it. Don't risk your safety by trying to put it out yourself.

Zion National Park is managed by the National Park Service, U.S. Department of the Interior. If you have any suggestions or comments about the Zion backcountry, please direct them to:

Superintendent
Zion National Park
Springdale, UT 84767-1099
(801) 772-3256

Remnants of superstructure on Cable Mountain.   *Victor L. Jackson as photographer*

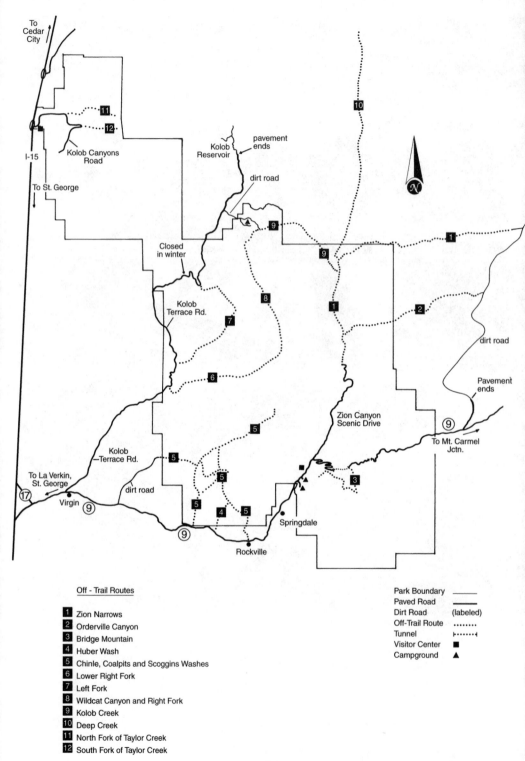

To Cedar City
To St. George
I-15
Kolob Canyons Road
To La Verkin, St. George
Virgin
Rockville
Springdale
To Mt. Carmel Jctn.
Kolob Reservoir
pavement ends
dirt road
Closed in winter
Kolob Terrace Rd.
Kolob Terrace Rd.
dirt road
Zion Canyon Scenic Drive
Pavement ends
dirt road
N

Off - Trail Routes

1 Zion Narrows
2 Orderville Canyon
3 Bridge Mountain
4 Huber Wash
5 Chinle, Coalpits and Scoggins Washes
6 Lower Right Fork
7 Left Fork
8 Wildcat Canyon and Right Fork
9 Kolob Creek
10 Deep Creek
11 North Fork of Taylor Creek
12 South Fork of Taylor Creek

Park Boundary ———
Paved Road ▬▬▬
Dirt Road (labeled)
Off-Trail Route ....
Tunnel ⊢·······⊣
Visitor Center ■
Campground ▲

The routes in this area are accessible from east of the Zion-Mt. Carmel Tunnel. St. Rt. 9 winds eastward and upward as it leaves Zion Canyon, passing through a world of crossbedded sandstone and weirdly eroded slickrock. The plateau beyond is heavily vegetated with ponderosa pine forest occurring in some locales. Dirt roads found east of the park provide access to a number of outstanding hiking routes including the well known Zion Narrows. All but one of the routes in this section begin outside Zion National Park.

1 THE ZION NARROWS
Via the North Fork

Introduction

Where the Virgin River enters Zion National Park, it has carved a chasm 2,000 feet (610 m) deep into the Markagunt Plateau. The river meanders 16 miles (26 km) through a storm-sculptured gorge of sandstone arches, grottoes, and soaring fluted walls. The route is the river bed; *there is no trail.* River currents are strong; once you have penetrated the canyon from its upper end, it is not easy to turn back. Good planning, equipment, and physical conditioning are essential for a successful trip.

About one-third of the total river volume comes from the North Fork; two thirds from Deep Creek. Hiking is more difficult downstream, where depths and current increase.

> **Permits/Restrictions:** Backcountry permits are required for trips through the length of the Narrows or its tributary canyons, even day trips. Overnight hikers will be assigned a designated campsite upon receiving the permit. Permits are limited in number and are issued on a first come first served basis. Even under optimum conditions small children cannot safely make this trip. It is suggested that hikers be 12 years or older; 56 inches (140 cm) or taller.

Difficulty

This is a strenuous trip even for experienced backpackers. The hike drops an average of 30 yards (27 m) per mile (1.6 km)—which is ten times as steep as that of the Colorado River in the Grand Canyon. Many hikers are dismayed when they discover the difficulty of this trip; others find that it is a more strenuous trip than they wanted to make. Although there is no trail, paths made by other hikers are intermittently found adjacent to the river bed. Avoid stepping on vegetation. Much of the hike is in the river itself—it will be to your benefit to do this hike when the river water runs clear.

The footing is uneven and the rocks are slippery, especially from Deep Creek down. A hiker once characterized the footing on this hike as "trying to walk on greased bowling balls." There is a lot of truth to that statement in certain portions of the hike.

Due to the uneven footing, this hike should be avoided if you have knee or ankle problems. Joint injuries are the most common problem on this hike, followed by hypothermia.

Most of the summer it is possible to do this hike without *having* to swim, although most first time hikers end up swimming to avoid difficult backtracking around the deeper spots. Under adverse river conditions swimming is unavoidable.

Equipment Needs

Use a *walking stick* as a stable "third leg" for river crossings, for feeling out pool depths, and for balance on slippery rocks. Comfortable, lightweight (when wet) *boots* are a plus; the ankle support and padding are greatly appreciated by day's end. Be prepared to swim. Chest-deep holes may occur even when water levels are low. Wet, sodden backpacks can become a liability—pack your belongings in sealed *plastic bags* inside your pack for protection and flotation.

Wear wool, polypropylene, or any *synthetic fabric* that wicks moisture away from the skin, thus keeping you warmer even when wet. Avoid wearing cotton T-shirts or jeans. Remember, the clothes you wear will get wet so bring *additional warm clothes* for camp or in case you are delayed. Extra food is welcome when your appetite increases due to your exertion level.

Avoid using *ropes* in the river; used improperly, they may pin a person underwater in currents.

Remember to bring extra plastic bags to pack out all your trash.

Recommended Maps

The line map on page 23 is adequate for this hike. The Zion National Park Topographic Map is recommended if you wish to take a topo. The starting point and first mile or so of the hike is not shown on the topo, but the terrain is gentle and the text material below sufficient to follow the route.

Camping/Time Required/Permits

Through-Day Hikes: Well-conditioned, experienced hikers can travel the length of the Narrows in about 12 hours; it takes longer if the water is deep or muddy. Through-day hikes should probably be avoided by first time Narrows hikers; many groups have spent cold nights huddled on a damp sandbar because they thought they could do the hike in one day.

Overnight Trips through the Narrows: A two-day hike through the Narrows allows more time for photography and leisurely exploration of side canyons. There are 12 campsites above the high water mark between Deep Creek and Big Springs which are assigned as part of the permit process. Unpredictable weather limits camping to one night in the canyon. Camping is prohibited in the canyon between Big Springs and the Temple of Sinawava. Overnight hikers start at Chamberlain's Ranch—no permits will be issued by the National Park Service to hike upstream to camp overnight.

Water Sources

Water can be taken directly from the Virgin River or its tributaries, but due to heavy public use and upstream livestock contamination, all water sources should be purified. Springs begin to appear after Deep Creek; they become more frequent after the "Grotto." Watch for poison ivy (on both sides of the river) at Big Springs.

Each hiker will need a quart or two of water to get from Chamberlain's Ranch to the first springs.

Season

Before June, the river is usually too high and too cold with snow melt for hiking. The best times to hike the Narrows are in late June, early July and late September; the National Park Service usually opens the Narrows to through-trip hikes in early June. Thunderstorms from mid-July through early September can cause dangerous flash floods. In September and October the short days make overnight trips safer than day hikes through the length of the canyon. After October, trips through the entire canyon require wet suits and special preparation. During the winter, snow closes the access road to Chamberlain's Ranch.

The long, hot days of midsummer are best for day hikes in the Narrows if thunderstorm activity is absent. Pick up your permit the evening before and enter the canyon at dawn; after late August it may take all the hours of daylight to complete the trip. Late season cold weather, shade, and chilly nights require **extra** dry, warm clothing to prevent hypothermia.

Although the water is cold, a rewarding time to take the trip can be during the first week of October when the fall colors are changing. The maple, boxelder and oak leaves turn bright red, orange and yellow.

Allow sufficient time (2-6 days) after a flood for the silty river water to clear. This assures better visibility in route finding and foot placement at the many tricky crossings.

In 1992 the National Park Service put strict limits on the number of persons who could hike downstream from Chamberlain's Ranch to the Temple of Sinawava. These measures were taken to both protect the canyon environment and to preserve a quality experience. A Narrows brochure is available at the Visitor Center which details the procedures for obtaining a permit, as well as tips on what to bring and what to wear for this strenuous hike.

Hypothermia: Long immersion in cold water can cool the body to dangerous levels. Hypothermia may occur quickly without the victim's awareness. Avoid cotton clothing and eat high energy food, especially sugars and starches, before you are chilled. Watch for these signs of hypothermia:

- Uncontrollable shivering
- Stumbling and poor coordination
- Confusion or slurred speech
- Disorientation
- Fatigue and weakness

If you recognize any signs of hypothermia, stop hiking and immediately replace wet clothing. Warm the victim with your own body, and a hot drink. A pre-warmed sleeping bag and shelter from breeze will help prevent further heat loss.

Flash floods: Narrow desert canyons are notorious for flash flooding. The North Fork of the Virgin River drains a large watershed. Remember, blue sky overhead does not eliminate the possibility of flooding caused by torrents of water from upstream. Thunderstorms are more common from mid-July through early September.

As you hike, watch for signs of past high water levels— water line stains on the rock walls. Look for places where you can climb above this level if you must escape a flood.

Signs of possible flash flooding:

- Increased debris in the water.
- Sudden changes in water clarity from translucent to muddy.
- Rising water levels or stronger currents.
- Buildup of thunderclouds or distant sounds of thunder; rainfall.
- An increasing roar of water up canyon.

The Starting Point

The Narrows starting point is reached via Chamberlain's Ranch, private property outside Zion National Park. The dirt and gravel road is accessible by passenger car only when dry and in good condition; during rainstorms and snow it is impassable even to four-wheel drive vehicles. Snow closes the access road after October. Two vehicles need to be used, or shuttle arrangements made, so that you have transportation when you complete the hike at the Temple of

Sinawava. Check at the Zion Lodge Transportation Desk or call 801-772-3213 for commercial shuttle service information.

From the Park East Entrance Station, drive east 2.5 miles (4 km) on St. Rt. 9. Turn left and continue 18 miles (29 km) to a wooden bridge that crosses the North Fork of the Virgin River. Turn left on a smaller dirt road just beyond the bridge; you will reach the gate of Chamberlain's Ranch in about .5 mile (.8 km). From Zion Canyon, allow 1-1/2 hours to drive to this point. You may drive about .5 mile (.8 km) further to where the dirt road crosses the river. The North Fork of the Virgin River is a small, winding creek at this point. Please respect the private land you cross, and close all gates. You must park before crossing the river.

The Route

From the parking area adjacent to the river crossing, follow the dirt road across the river. The landowners ask visitors to not drive the narrow ranch road beyond this point.

The road parallels the river among irrigated pastures, a pastoral scene not indicative of the hike ahead. About 1.5 miles (2.4 km) from the parking area you pass Bulloch's Cabin, a rustic log cabin depicted on the Zion topographic map.

A short distance beyond, the character of the route begins to change. The road ends; a rough bulldozer track goes further, but also soon ends. You begin to make multiple stream crossings (the water is quite nippy early on a summer morning.)

Note that the top of the Navajo Sandstone appears and a gradual narrowing of the valley has occurred. The canyon walls gain height. This area just downstream from Bulloch's Cabin is still private land.

Continue downstream. The river weaves across land administered by the State of Utah, the Bureau of Land Management (the North Fork Wilderness Study Area) and the National Park Service.

After continually crossing and recrossing the small stream, you arrive at several narrow passageways. Simon Gulch, named after a local pioneer, is a side canyon draining from the north. It is located 4.9 miles (7.9 km) past Bulloch's Cabin just before the stream takes a jog to the left.

Eventually you reach a 12-foot (3.7 m) waterfall 6.6 miles (10.6 km) from the start of the hike. Fortunately, a narrow cleft passageway up and to the left allows you to circumvent the spectacular falls.

Following the stream another 1.4 miles (2.3 km), you come to an open area—the confluence of North Fork and Deep Creek. Deep Creek adds about 60% of the total volume to the river. Deep Creek is normally a couple degrees colder, and clearer than the North Fork. Downstream, the river is augmented by numerous seeps and springs, Kolob Creek, Goose Creek, and Orderville Canyon. Keep track of your progress by recognizing these side canyons. As the river gets deeper, it becomes more important to choose your crossing and wading spots carefully. Seek shallow areas in slow moving water; level stretches with several channels; or wide places with small ripples all the way across. Be alert to dangers downstream. Do not cross directly above cascades or rough, rocky areas with swift-moving water. Look for alternatives; you can avoid most obstacles and deep spots. Angle downstream; never fight the current. Remember to unfasten the waist strap on your backpack when wading swift or deeper sections of river; a tightly-fastened pack cannot be shed quickly and is danger-ous if the current sweeps you off your feet.

Kolob Creek enters on the right 1.6 miles (2.6 km) below the con-fluence of Deep Creek and North Fork. Kolob Creek may be dry due to water storage in Kolob Reservoir. Late summer will often see a cold water flow added to the river here as the dam releases water for downstream irrigation users.

.7 mile (1.1 km) below the "Grotto" is a narrow, often missed scenic side canyon named Goose Creek. This canyon offers an inter-esting side hike. Travel down from the top is technical—there are several rappels. At the head of the canyon is the tiny Goose Creek Wilderness Study Area (BLM). Below Goose Creek there are a few small patches of poison ivy growing adjacent to some of the hiker paths. Know what it looks like and avoid this plant. Very few per-sons have been bothered by it—perhaps because the irritating oils are washed off during river crossings downstream. The next major land-mark is Big Springs. A cascading waterfall pours clear water through luxuriant plant growth into the river. The last of the scarce poison ivy grows here on both sides of the river. Big Springs is a good water re-supply point, although the river is rushing in front of it and access can be an adventure when water levels are higher.

Big Springs marks the beginning of a 3-mile (4.8 km) section of narrows where sheer sandstone cliffs limit escape from flash flood; hold off going any further if rain is imminent. This is a good location to assess your condition; the obstacles, crossings, and hiking get more difficult from here downstream. Gear should be wrapped or bagged—the deepest pools lie ahead! From Big Springs down the Virgin River is closed to camping. For the next 3.0 miles (4.8 km) there are no safe camping spots; after that you enter a day use area with considerable upstream day hiker traffic. Travel in the dark below Big Springs is difficult with a flashlight; impossible without one.

This section of the Narrows is amazing. 2000-foot (610 m) vertical rock walls towering overhead, the river filling the canyon from wall to wall, high arches, delicate plant life struggling to survive; all pro-vide lifelong memories.

The deepest pools that you must navigate on this hike are found in this area. Go slowly, using your hiking staff to find the shallowest route. Typically the deepest spot is waist to chest deep; under rare conditions you may have to swim. There are shallower routes around most deep spots if you take the time to find them.

2.1 miles (3.4 km) downstream a narrow barren passageway opens to the east from which a small stream emerges. This is Orderville Canyon, the destination for most upstream-bound day hikers.

1.3 miles (2.1 km) further you will wonder at a narrow, ribbonlike stream that slides down the east canyon wall from Mystery Canyon. 80 yards (70 m) further is the paved Riverside Walk which takes you 1.0 mile (1.6 km) to the end point of this route at the Temple of Sinawava Parking Area.

You are back to "civilization"!

Zion Narrows Via the North Fork - Distance Chart

	mi	km
(S) Chamberlain's river crossing (parking)	0	0
Bulloch's Cabin	1.5	2.4
Simon Gulch	4.9	7.9
Falls	6.9	11.1
Deep Creek	8.0	12.9
Kolob Creek	8.9	14.3
"Grotto" alcove	9.5	15.3
Goose Creek	10.1	16.3
Big Springs	10.8	17.4
Orderville Canyon	12.9	20.8
Mystery Canyon Falls	14.2	22.9
Riverside Walk	14.7	23.7
(E) Temple of Sinawava (parking)	15.7	25.3

Use with the Zion National Park Topographic Map

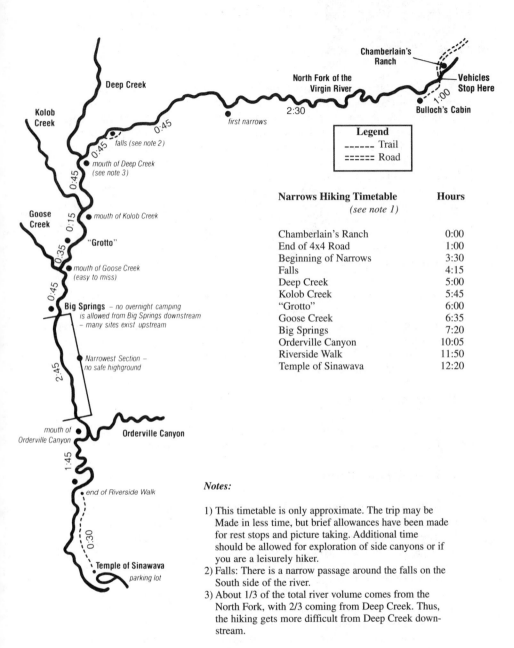

Legend

------ Trail
====== Road

Narrows Hiking Timetable *(see note 1)*	Hours
Chamberlain's Ranch	0:00
End of 4x4 Road	1:00
Beginning of Narrows	3:30
Falls	4:15
Deep Creek	5:00
Kolob Creek	5:45
"Grotto"	6:00
Goose Creek	6:35
Big Springs	7:20
Orderville Canyon	10:05
Riverside Walk	11:50
Temple of Sinawava	12:20

Notes:

1) This timetable is only approximate. The trip may be
Made in less time, but brief allowances have been made
for rest stops and picture taking. Additional time
should be allowed for exploration of side canyons or if
you are a leisurely hiker.
2) Falls: There is a narrow passage around the falls on the
South side of the river.
3) About 1/3 of the total river volume comes from the
North Fork, with 2/3 coming from Deep Creek. Thus,
the hiking gets more difficult from Deep Creek downstream.

2 ORDERVILLE CANYON
From the North Fork Road Downstream

Introduction/Difficulty

Spectacular narrow Orderville Canyon, which flows into the lower portion of the Zion Narrows, can be a very difficult canyon to hike. Orderville Canyon is known for its slippery clay mud; obstacles can include small waterfalls, big logjams, and pools. This canyon is subject to radical change due to the effects of violent flash floods.

You should be in good physical condition and have some prior canyoneering experience before attempting this route. Those hiking this canyon should be prepared to wade (or swim occasionally) and should possess basic rope use skills for the one significant obstacle.

Orderville Canyon is named for the Mormon pioneer town of Orderville, located about ten miles east as the crow flies.

Equipment Needs

A 50-foot (15 m) climbing rope and rappelling gear will be needed. Experienced canyoneers may choose to leave the rappelling gear and downclimb the rope. A sturdy hiking staff is recommended, especially when the Virgin River is reached. Waterproof the gear inside your pack with plastic bags. Backcountry permits are required for all trips through Orderville Canyon.

Recommended Maps

Clear Creek Mountain, UT (USGS 7.5' quad); see page 29.
Temple of Sinawava, UT (USGS 7.5' quad); see page 30.

Camping/Time Required

Orderville Canyon is usually done as a long day hike. The canyon offers only slim possibilities for camping, and is closed to camping for the last mile. The Virgin River is closed to camping from Big Springs downstream. Keep flash flood safety in mind if you do camp. All precautions pertaining to the Zion Narrows (pages 16–23) also apply to Orderville Canyon.

In the upstream area east of Bulloch Gulch are some narrow benches where small, sloping camps may be fit between the trees. Most will be crowded with two people.

There are several side canyons which invite exploration, but first time hikers should not take long side trips during a day trip through Orderville Canyon; the obstacles past Bulloch Gulch may require considerable time.

Water Sources

Orderville Canyon is usually (hopefully!) dry above Bulloch Gulch. Spring flow below Bulloch Gulch may supply your drinking water needs with purification or treatment.

Season

Summer is the best time to hike Orderville Canyon. The Zion Narrows are occasionally closed when bad weather threatens; Orderville Canyon will also close, as it is part of that river system. Orderville Canyon has a large number of maples which provide fantastic color contrast with the grey rock during October.

The Starting Point

From the East Entrance Station, drive east on St. Rt. 9 just 2.5 miles (4 km) to the North Fork County Road. Turn left (only the first 3 miles are paved) and drive north for 12.7 miles (20.5 km) to the Orderville Gulch culvert. Do not attempt the drive to Orderville Canyon when the road is wet or rain threatens; even 4-wheel drive vehicles have been stuck or stranded in the mud here. You may begin the hike at the culvert, but an easier approach is found by backtracking in your vehicle .8 mile (1.3 km) to where a dirt road turns right (west) on the crest of a small hill. On the east side of the North Fork Road is a network of roads; the westbound road you want has thick Gambel oak to either side. Follow it a short distance to a wire corral area. 2-wheel drive vehicles stop here; 4-wheel drives may continue to the valley bottom, cutting about 1.5 miles off the start of the hike. Respect the property you are crossing; it is an unmarked mingling of BLM and private land.

The Route

Hikers (or 4-wheel drives) should follow the rough road downhill through the Gambel oak forest. Another faint 4-wheel drive track intersects our road from the left. Continue west and downhill, following the double-rutted road another .8 mile (1.3 km) to the bottom of Orderville Gulch, then across the meager stream. Continue following this road, along the right bank of the stream, for .4 mile (.6 km). Continue as the road crosses the stream to the left bank. 4-wheel drives will have to stop about 100 yards (90 m) after the stream crossing.

The road diminishes to a cow path leading through tall rabbit brush. The path becomes faint just after a prominent canyon enters the valley from the left. Follow the path in the same general direction through the rabbit brush about 200 yards (180 m) and drop off the flat bench into the streambed. Follow the streambed .6 mile (1 km) to the beginning of Orderville Canyon, at the top of a 125-foot (38m) dryfall. The streambed is usually dry for the next couple of miles (3 km) in the summer. This is also the start of the Orderville Wilderness Study Area, BLM wild land adjacent to Zion National Park.

The dryfall is most easily bypassed to the left. Simply go back upstream a short distance, then walk south to one of several places which lead down the steep landslide slopes, overgrown with willow, onto a bench. Follow the bench south and parallel to the main streambed to where it is easy to drop into the canyon bottom near the drainage entering from the left (south.) There is a major Mancos Shale landslide here and the clay muds are apparent. From here on the route is located in the streambed.

Walk down the canyon .4 mile (.7 km) to Birch Hollow, a drainage entering from the left via a spectacular—usually dry—waterfall. It is worthwhile to scramble up to the base of the fall to examine the interesting carvings formed by centuries of falling water. An interesting chockstone is lodged high above at the top of the fall.

During the next .6 mile (1 km), pass several minor side canyons, some small benches that might make steep campsites, and an interesting alcove on the left before arriving at Walker Gulch which enters from the right and has a sheer wall at the mouth. This side canyon was named for Levi Walker, an early settler.

Some of the side canyons shown on the topo map are easy to miss, as the entire drainage is often not visible from the bottom of Orderville Canyon.

In the next .9 mile (1.5 km) several small drainages enter the deepening canyon; you will pass through a narrows and then arrive at Esplin Gulch, named for a family of early settlers and stockmen who lived in this vicinity. It is a major drainage entering Orderville Canyon from the north, with a small easily-missed mouth, and offers an interesting side hike. The plateau area above Orderville Canyon is wild and rugged; wildlife also use the canyon in their travel. Black bear and mountain lion tracks were photographed here in 1985.

After Esplin Gulch, walk by a minor left-hand canyon, an open area on the right, a small couloir, and a set of narrows. The unmarked boundary into Zion National Park is located in the middle of these narrows. It is easy to get confused—just keep heading downstream! In these narrows you arrive at the major obstacle on this hike, a large boulder in the streambed which has created a dam and dryfall. This 15- foot (5 m) high fall may be downclimbed or chimneyed to the right if it is dry, although it is still very slippery. It is safer to carefully anchor a hand line around a boulder on the left and climb or rappel down.

Continuing down the streambed, you pass a righthand canyon, a dry waterfall alcove on the left, a short section of narrows, then a crevice-type drainage on the left. After about .3 mile (.5 km) a couloir on the left is graced with a flying buttress arch which seems to be leaning against, rather than connected to, the rock. It is worth looking for, but difficult to see under certain light conditions.

The next major canyon enters on the left .7 mile (1.1 km) from the arch just passed. This unnamed canyon is easily identified by the 20-foot (6 m) high dryfall created by a large chockstone, about 40 yards (37 m) south of the Orderville drainage.

Continuing down Orderville, you pass a beautiful narrows, a fracture which crosses the canyon, a drainage, and more narrows. The streambed will become muddy with meager water seepage.

Bulloch Gulch, named for another early settler, enters from the right and carries a small amount of water. Adjectives fail to describe the overwhelming beauty of this area, and cameras fail to capture the entirety of the grandeur.

Below Bulloch Gulch, the small flow in the canyon bottom increases gradually. A canyon entering from the left soon adds a small amount. Soon an incredible narrows is entered. Immediately after the narrows is an interesting geologic feature—two huge fracture drainages which cross the canyon perpendicularly. These two parallel fractures follow the natural north-south fracture lines evident elsewhere in the park, but are seen vividly here. In the second fracture, about 50 yards (40 m) south, is an interesting double chocks/one-arch-waterfall. There is usually a small trickle of water coming down this left drainage.

Just past the two fractures, the stream appears to have done the impossible—by carving a slit through a tall monolithic wall, leaving the walls only a few yards apart. Soon after these breathtaking narrows can be a major obstacle: two gargantuan boulders, one forming a dam and waterfall, the other a mammoth chockstone braced above and against both canyon walls. Bypass the obstacle to the left or right, depending on the state of the debris and the height of the drop. It is safest to anchor your rope to the firmly wedged driftwood logs and downclimb. The drop is about 15 feet (5 m).

Next, go through another narrows and easily pass to the right of a house-sized boulder. Look up to glimpse white slickrock high above—the south shoulder of Wynopits Mountain. Next pass four huge boulders, then arrive at a large boulder which channels the stream into a small funnel emptying into a pool. If filled with floating debris, it can be quite treacherous; if so, lower yourself off a 10-foot (3 m) drop to the left of the boulder.

Past the pool, go through a narrows which forms a huge bend to the right forming an alcove. Before long, arrive at the top of a small waterfall and pool. The pool can be chest deep depending on conditions; rig a rope if necessary.

Continue another 100 yards (90 m) to the top of a pretty 7-foot (2 m) waterfall. Stay to the left on the slimy rock. Face the rock while carefully downclimbing on some slippery toeholds in the rock.

Several minor obstacles remain. They may be bypassed with little difficulty as the canyon opens and seeps and springs become numerous. After another brief narrows, you arrive at the confluence of Orderville Canyon and the North Fork of the Virgin River, (see page 23). Walk downstream to the paved Riverside Walk and the parking area at the Temple of Sinawava.

Orderville Canyon - Distance Chart

	mi	km
(S) Begin hike, wire corral trailhead	0	0
Enter valley	1.1	1.8
4-wheel drive road ends	1.7	2.7
Drop off bench, follow streambed	2.5	4.0
125-foot (38 m) dryfall	3.1	5.0
Birch Hollow dryfall	3.7	6.0
Walker Gulch	4.4	7.1
Esplin Gulch	5.4	8.7
15-foot boulder obstacle (boundary area)	5.9	9.5
Flying buttress arch	6.7	10.8
Bulloch Gulch	7.9	12.7
Two parallel fractures	8.3	13.4
10-foot (3 m) fall and pool	8.9	14.4
Cascade with toeholds	9.2	14.8
Orderville/North Fork Confluence	9.7	15.6
Riverside Walk	11.5	18.5
(E) Temple of Sinawava	12.5	20.2

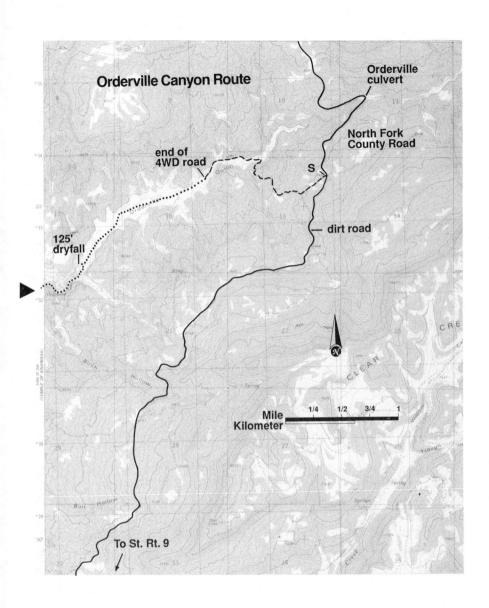

Orderville Canyon Route

Orderville culvert

North Fork County Road

end of 4WD road

S

dirt road

125' dryfall

Mile
Kilometer

1/4   1/2   3/4   1

To St. Rt. 9

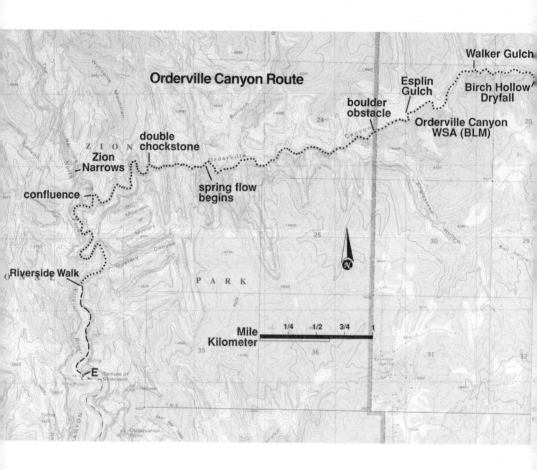

Orderville Canyon Route

Walker Gulch

Esplin Gulch

Birch Hollow Dryfall

boulder obstacle

Orderville Canyon WSA (BLM)

double chockstone

Zion Narrows

spring flow begins

confluence

Riverside Walk

E

Mile
Kilometer

1/4   1/2   3/4   1

The presence of live streams in Zion's desert enviroment contributes to the park's mysteries and attraction.

3 BRIDGE MOUNTAIN ARCH
Via Gifford Canyon and Hepworth Wash

Introduction/Difficulty

This strenuous, trail-less hike requires some Class IV climbing and belay work. It should be attempted only by those with well developed route finding/map reading abilities. Because this is a round trip hike, hikers should carefully observe the landmarks behind them so that they are not confused on the return route. Difficulties include numerous ascents and descents, friction scrambling on slickrock, walking in loose sand and scree, bushwhacking, and climbing a short Class IV chimney. Weather conditions may add to the difficulty.

Equipment Needs

Those contemplating this hike will need comfortable boots, a 150 foot (50 m) climbing rope, seat harnesses, and possibly some 1" tubular webbing.

Recommended Maps

Zion National Park Topographic Map (ZNHA); see page 35.

Camping/Time Required

Although the hike may be completed as a long one-day round trip, some will choose to camp overnight in Hepworth Wash and get an early start the next day for the arch. Nine hours will be required by those in excellent condition, but 10–16 hours will be required by most groups making this hike for the first time.

Water Sources

If attempting the hike during warmer months, at least one gallon of water per hiker per day is recommended. An unreliable brackish seep in Hepworth Wash offers a possible source of water. Many hikers carry extra water initially, then cache it for the return trip.

Season

Blistering temperatures, coupled with the sun's rays reflecting off bare white sandstone, should discourage prudent hikers from attempting this hike during the hot months. Cooler days of spring or fall are suggested; long dry periods during winter may make this trip possible during the cooler months. This route is not feasible when snow or ice patches are present east of the Zion-Mt. Carmel Tunnel.

The Starting Point

Drive to the east end of the Zion-Mt. Carmel Tunnel on St. Rt. 9 and park at the Canyon Overlook Trail Parking Area.

The Route

Scramble down from the parking lot into Pine Creek Wash below the restroom building. Walk up the main wash about 25 yards (25 m), then scramble up the slickrock slope to the left of the Gifford Canyon dryfall. As you get up in the trees, follow a faint path, then make a right turn passing in front (north) of the broken butte guarding the entrance to Gifford Canyon. Walk up very straight Gifford Canyon about .8 mile (1.3 km).

Now the work begins! The route to Bridge Mountain leaves Gifford Canyon headed west and climbs up the slickrock, working through a set of ledges, keeping under and to the south of a small prominent dome on the skyline. Exact route selection in this area is partly personal preference and partly luck. The easiest route through the ledges will be found by veering to the left (south) as you near their base. It is easy to get skunked due to unseen obstacles and have to backtrack; be persistent.

After gaining some 705 feet (215 m) in elevation, you will enter a large amphitheater-like bowl. Head west, but stay right of the drainage. As you near the head of the bowl, the easiest route to the

Descent route into west-flowing canyon, from sandflat (plateau) to Hepworth Wash.

33

plateau lies on the south side of the bowl where the ledges are more broken.

After reaching the scenic, sandflat plateau, you will have to go north to enter the proper west-flowing canyon, which is located between peak 6631 and peak 6500+ (by contour lines.)

Descend into the head of this canyon, which is bowl-shaped at its head, by the route of your choice. As you arrive near the bottom of the bowl, climb up 213 feet (65 m) to the north to a fin with some hoodoos on it (instead of following the streambed down the canyon). A rock cairn has been erected on a saddle between the hoodoos, though there is no guarantee it will always be there. There is some Class II climbing to reach the saddle. From the cairn or saddle, make your way down to the canyon bottom, staying to the left side of the large couloir and losing 100 yards (90 m) in elevation. Once in the bottom follow the canyon down to where it joins Hepworth Wash.

A slow brackish seep can be found 300 yards (274 m) to the south up Hepworth Wash. Follow the wash up to where you find a small pool of poor quality water in the wash bottom. This seep is more reliable in spring and fall than in summer. It must be well treated before drinking. A large sandy area to the south makes a nice campsite.

Our route to the arch now follows Hepworth Wash to the north (downstream) past the canyon which drains westwardly from peak 6631. Just past this canyon and wash is a wash draining east from Bridge Mountain. Leave Hepworth Wash and walk in a northwest direction by the easiest route to the first couloir north of Bridge Mountain.

Ascend the couloir to the notch divide, then go steeply down the north side of the couloir 150 yards (140 m) to where a scree and oak-covered bench is taken to the left. After a 25-yard (23 meter) traverse, swing left and up slightly, then around a corner to the base of a 30-

Looking roughly north, first couloir north of Bridge Mountian.

Bridge Mountain

Route to the arch

34

foot (9 m) chimney. Here an experienced climber leads, then belays the others or sets up a handline. A fall here could be fatal—use caution. Natural anchors can be used.

After climbing the chimney (which is rappelled or belayed on the return trip) continue up the difficult Class III fracture another 100 yards (100 m). Turn right, not climbing more than 8 yards (7 m) higher, and traverse westwardly.

Drop down 35 yards (32 m) into a secluded hanging valley and walk south toward the grove of quaking aspen. From the aspen, stay at the same elevation and traverse over scree and slickrock less than 200 yards (175 m) to the delicately structured natural arch.

Reverse the route to return to the Canyon Overlook Parking Area.

Bridge Mountain Arch - Distance Chart

	mi	km
(S) Canyon Overlook Parking Area	0	0
Leave Gifford Canyon	.8	1.3
Sandflat (plateau)	1.6	2.6
Hepworth Wash	2.5	4.0
Top of couloir	4.3	6.9
Chimney	4.5	7.3
Bridge Mountain Arch	5.0	8.1
(E) Canyon Overlook Parking Area	10.0	16.2

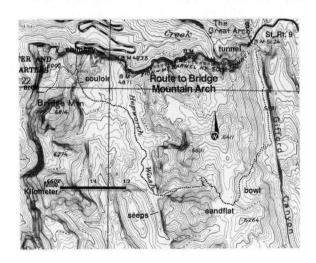

Bridge Mountain as seen from the Zion Canyon Visitor Center.

Kolob Arch in La Verkin Creek Drainage

Brian Chan

Tom Brereton

In the "Grand Alcove," Right Fork of North Creek, Route #8

 Differential erosion of sandstone

39

Tom Brereton

Hiking the Narrows, Route #1

James Dunaway   *The South Fork of Taylor Creek, Route #12*

Arch on Bridge Mountain, Rt. #3
Inset: Chimney on the route to Bridge
Mountain Arch, Route #3
Opposite: Just upstream from the "Subway,"
Left Fork of North Creek, Route #7.

Tom Bereton

Victor Jackson

Tom Brereton

"Barrier Falls," Right Fork of North Creek, Route #8 or #6

Tom Brereton

West Temple (left) and Mt. Kinesava as seen from the west.

This 12,000 acre corner of Zion National Park has the lowest elevation (3,640 feet/1,109 m) in the park, experiences the warmest temperatures, and gets the most sunshine. Thus it has the most desert-like environment in Zion, with plants and animals adapted to water conserving and heat avoidance lifestyles.

Easily accessible from St. Rt. 9 near the town of Rockville, it is quiet and offers a different hiking experience from the rest of Zion. The views of Mt. Kinesava, the West Temple, and Cougar Mountain change dramatically with location and time of day. If you visit Zion during the spring, fall or winter, consider exploring this delightful area!

4 **Huber Wash**
and the "Petrified Logjam"

Introduction/Difficulty

Although this hike is trail-less, the easy walking in the bed of Huber Wash makes the hike just slightly more difficult than the maintained trails of Zion Canyon. The gentle wash bottom rises slowly for two miles, gaining only about 100 yards (100 m) in elevation.

Equipment Needs

No special equipment is needed for this route.

Recommended Maps

Zion National Park Topographic Map (ZNHA); see page 48.

Camping/Time Required

This leisurely cross-country stroll may be completed in a two and one-half hour round trip. If you wish to extend this trip for other exploration, you may camp along the Chinle Trail beyond the "Petrified Logjam."

Water Sources

Hikers will find no reliable source of water, although small seeps are sometimes found during the wettest months

Season

It is extremely hot here during the summer months; the cooler portion of the year is the best time to visit. Due to the low elevation and southern exposure, it may be completed during the coldest months when most other backcountry areas are inaccessible.

The Starting Point

Drive one mile west of Rockville on St. Rt. 9 to the first wash, where a road sign designates "Huber Wash." Drive 100 yards (90 m) back toward Rockville and park at the first gate. This access road is found 6 miles (9.7 km) from the South Entrance.

The Route

Go through the roadside gate and begin walking north paralleling Huber Wash by following the power line access road east of the wash. The land between the highway and the park boundary is owned by the State of Utah which leases the grazing rights. Leave all gates in this area shut. As you approach the park boundary .4 mile (.6 km) from the paved road, drop into and follow the wash.

There is a hikers' gate in the boundary fence a few yards west of the wash. From here the route is simple; just follow the wash as it winds and meanders eventually to the northeast. Two of the largest meanders may be avoided by shortcutting across the adjacent benches. Look for small pieces of petrified wood in the streambed, but leave them for others to enjoy.

As you proceed upstream the Shinarump conglomerate, the caprock on the mesas above, appears closer until the canyon narrows and you are stopped by a dryfall. The layer exposing the Petrified Logjam is up on the wall to the right. Climb the talus to get a good view.

This ledge is definitely interesting and worth the effort to get here. Thoughtless hikers may be tempted to break park regulations by taking pieces of petrified wood (not of gem quality) for souvenirs, but it should not be disturbed. Let others view it and wonder.

To get up to the Chinle, backtrack roughly 100 yards (90 m) downstream, then work your way up among the boulders on the north side of the wash (opposite the logjam to a relatively narrow and easy chimney by which the mesa above can be accessed. Backpacks may have to be passed up individually.

Head northeast paralleling Huber Wash by any convenient route until the Chinle Trail is reached.

Huber Wash - Chinle Trail—Distance Chart

	mi	km
(S) St. Rt. 9	0	0
Park Boundary Fence	.4	.6
Petrified Logjam	2.3	3.7
Petrified Forest plateau	2.5	4.0
(E) Chinle Trail	3.0	4.8

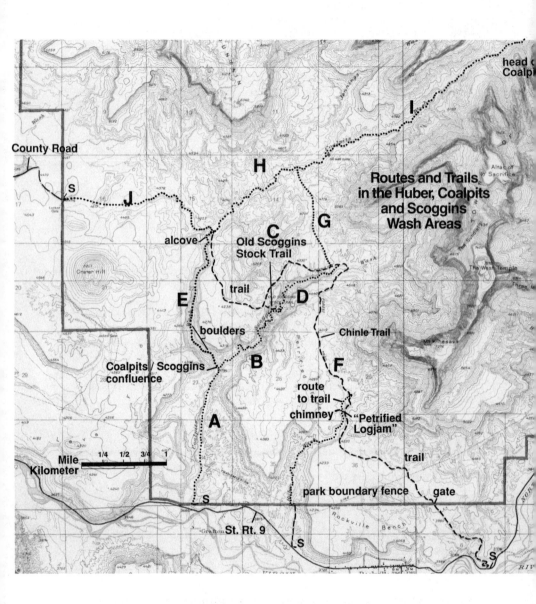

head of
Coalpi

County Road

I

H

Routes and Trails
in the Huber, Coalpits
and Scoggins
Wash Areas

J

S

alcove

C

Old Scoggins
Stock Trail

G

trail

E

D

boulders

Chinle Trail

Coalpits / Scoggins
confluence

B

F

route
to trail

A

chimney

"Petrified
Logjam"

Mile
Kilometer

1/4 1/2 3/4 1

trail

park boundary fence

gate

S

St. Rt. 9

LS

S

Petrified logs at "Logjam" Huber Wash   *Victor L. Jackson*

Introduction/Difficulty

These routes are organized differently from other sections of this book. The terrain in the Coalpits and Scoggins Wash area is more moderate than in much of Zion. You can travel just about anywhere you want to go if you are persistent in trying to get there—but there are some traveled routes which can be linked together to create a trip matching your needs.

The main difficulty encountered in these areas will be lack of developed trails. The ground is generally rolling with uneven surfaces and rocky footing in places.

You should be able to interpret and read topographic maps if you want to navigate by these routes.

Equipment Needs

No special gear is needed. Take a topo map and be able to read it.

Recommended Maps

Zion National Park Topographic Map (ZNHA); see page 48.

Camping/Time Required

Hikers do all kinds of trips into this area—day, overnight, and multi-day hikes—depending on their time schedules.

There are many areas suitable for campsites throughout the area. The Park Service recommends you choose previously-used sites or areas of bare soil to localize impacts. Vegetation is slow to recover if disturbed in this desert area.

The most popular places to camp are along Coalpits Wash, where there is a reliable stream. Shade can be found under occasional cottonwoods or nearby junipers. There are numerous dry (but scenic!) campsite locations on the plateaus above the washes. Camping is not allowed from St. Rt. 9 to 1 mile (1.6 km) beyond the park boundry.

Water Sources

Coalpits Wash sports a small but reliable stream. There is a small spring located a few feet from the stream in an alcove about 150 yards (140 m) downstream from where the Chinle Trail ends in Coalpits Wash. Other small spring seepage areas can be found at the head of Coalpits Wash and at the head of Terry and Jennings Washes. Scoggins Wash occasionally carries a tiny stream of water during wet spring months.

Season

This is a great off-season hiking area. Avoid it during the summer! Perhaps the best months to hike here are November, and February through May during stable weather. December and January are beautiful if no snow is present and the weather is mild.

After a saturating rain or snow, clay muds can clump up on your boots, making it slippery and difficult to get around. Walking at these times also does resource damage to desert soil surfaces.

The Starting Points

Chinle Trailhead: Located 3.5 miles (5.6 km) south of the park's South Entrance Station at mile marker 29 on St. Rt. 9. This trail is a main access to this area and several routes may connect with it. Please respect the private property from St. Rt. 9 to the park boundary. Pedestrian use only—bicyles prohibited.

Huber Wash: Discussed in the previous chapter, see page 46.

Coalpits Wash: Located 7.4 miles (11.9 km) from the South Entrance Station on St. Rt. 9, designated by a road sign. A dirt parking area is located on the east side of Coalpits Wash north of St. Rt. 9. A "pass through gate" allows hikers by without climbing the boundary fence. This is the primary access point for most hikers to this area.

Crater Hill Parking Area: This little-used entry provides the shortest and quickest access to upper Coalpits Wash if you have a 4-wheel drive or high clearance vehicle. From the South Entrance Station Drive 12.7 miles (20.5 km) west on St. Rt. 9. Turn right (north) onto the county dirt road known as the "Dalton Wash Road" (no sign) located about .6 mile (1 km) west of the "101 Rancho." Follow the main dirt road 3.8 miles (6.1 km) northeast paralleling Dalton Wash. (Don't take this road in wet, muddy or snowy conditions; it will be impassable at a scary spot near the head of Dalton Wash.) The road finally climbs out of Dalton Wash; it is not maintained the final .7 mile (1.1 km) to the parking area and hiker gate at the park boundary.

The Routes and Distances

Note: Route letter designations are keyed to map on p. 48.

A—Coalpits Parking Area to Coalpits/Scoggins Confluence 1.8 miles (2.9 km)

This is the most frequently used entry to this area. After passing through the boundary fence, follow the open Coalpits Wash valley to its confluence with Scoggins Wash. Coalpits Wash carries a small stream of water, although it sometimes dries up during the summer months. There is no developed trail up Coalpits Wash, though there are well beaten paths that are easily followed. The most-traveled path is found on the east side of the wash on the terrace level back from the creek.

B—Coalpits/Scoggins Confluence to the Old Scoggins Stock Trail
    (Scoggins Wash)
    1.5 mile (2.4 km)

It is an easy walk up the bottom of Scoggins Wash. Usually dry, the wash winds up the canyon, flat-bottomed with some rocks and holes. There are pretty cross-cuts in the canyon walls. A small back-country sign on the left (north) bank marks the start of the Old Scoggins Stock Trail.

C—Old Scoggins Stock Trail*
    .3 mile (.5 km)

This short trail was built by pioneers to move their livestock from the lowland to the mesas above. While it has deteriorated, it is the most practical way up the cliffs. It is marked by signs at the Scoggins Wash and Chinle Trail ends.

D—Old Scoggins Stock Trail to Chinle Trail
    (via the Scoggins Wash bottom)
    1.0 mile (1.6 km)

This section of Scoggins Wash gets narrower and rougher. You should work around the large boulders. Footing is irregular with many rocks; the wash bottom is uneven. This is a small, interesting canyon. Watch for the Chinle Trail if you plan to connect with it; there is no sign and the crossing is not well defined.

E—Coalpits/Scoggins Confluence to alcove spring
   (via Coalpits Wash)
   1.6 mile (2.6 km)

This area is described by many hikers as the most attractive section of Coalpits Wash. The small creek gurgles through gargantuan boulders, forming pretty pools, cascades and small waterfalls. You can follow the creek up the canyon to where the spring is found in the alcove, but it will take you a considerable amount of time. There is a path of sorts, mostly on the left (west) bank of the wash which avoids most of the chaos in the stream bottom. There are very few campsites in this area.

F—Park boundary fence to Coalpits Wash
   (via Chinle Trail)*
   6.8 miles (11 km)

This trail is a pleasant and scenic walk taking the hiker to the middle of the Coalpits Wash drainage near the alcove spring, found about 150 yards (140 m) downstream from the trail's end. A small, pretty waterfall is found about 50 yards (46 m) downstream from the end of the trail.

G—Chinle Trail (north of Scoggins) to Oil Well Ruins in Coalpits Wash
   1.1 mile (1.8 km)

Leave the Chinle Trail about .4 mile (.6 km) west of where it crosses the head of Scoggins Wash. This is a shortcut route to Coalpits Wash via a saddle that connects the Coalpits and Scoggins drainages. Head north, staying to the right (east) of the dry wash drainage. It is very easy walking initially. Head toward the low point between the hills, avoiding the many small ravines and washes as you get further from the Chinle Trail. Bear to the right (east) in the saddle area. Survey the steep slopes, then traverse a route down to Coalpits Wash, avoiding the steepest bluffs. You may need to hike upstream to the oil well ruins which are located about 300 yards (270 m) downstream from the Jennings/Coalpits confluence on the south banks of the wash.

*For more information, see *Zion—The Trails*

H—Chinle Trail End (Coalpits Wash) to Jennings/Coalpits
 Confluence
 2.5 miles (4 km)

This is a pleasant walk along the winding creek. Cottonwoods and
a few ponderosa pine grow along the creek; there are numerous
campsite areas. The oil well ruins are located about 2.3 miles (3.7 km)
from the end of the Chinle Trail. Please don't camp in this historic
site. Jennings Wash comes into Coalpits from the north, usually car-
rying a small stream of water.

I—Jennings/Coalpits Confluence to head of Coalpits Wash
 4.0 miles (6.5 km)

If you want to get away from people, this area has good possibilities. Relatively few hikers get this far up Coalpits Wash. Paths are
less worn and the willows get thick along the bottom in places; use
the creek as your guide and it will lead you nearer to the spectacular
cliffs so visible throughout the area—the Altar of Sacrifice, the
Towers of the Virgin, and other magnificent crags found at the head
of the Coalpits Wash drainage.

J—Crater Hill Parking Area to Coalpits Wash
 (near alcove spring)
 2.2 miles (3.5 km)

This is a basic cross-country route which parallels the small, dry
drainage that begins south of the parking area. The wash becomes a
main drainage as it passes east of the hill found about .5 mile (.8 km)
from the parking area. The route is not as straightforward as it
looks—there are many smaller washes and hills that don't show up
on the topographic map. But it is still the fastest access to upper
Coalpits Wash. The drainage you follow and parallel eventually emp-
ties into Coalpits Wash about 100 yards (90 m) upstream from the
alcove spring.

*For more information, see *Zion—The Trails*

The Kolob Terrace area is one of the least known treasures of Zion. This less-developed area is accessible via the paved Kolob Terrace Road which heads north from the town of Virgin, Utah located on St. Rt. 9, 14 miles (22.6 km) west of the South Entrance. A small primitive campground is located near Lava Point Lookout; no water is available. Park inholdings—parcels of privately-owned land—are located within this section of the park. You will see cattle and cabins adjacent to the road.

The array of canyon hikes in this area of the park is outstanding. All have flash-flooding problems during big storms; most have obstacles that can be difficult to pass. But there are many rewards for the careful hiker!

Introduction/Difficulty

The Right Fork of North Creek is relatively unknown despite its colorful beauty. There are a number of beautiful pools suitable for swims, dramatic waterfalls, and scenery that won't quit on this hike. "Barrier Falls" is the farthest upstream you can hike; plan to return on the same route. Hikers should have some basic route finding experience since the return trip exits through the lava cliffs and can be difficult to locate.

Equipment Needs

Climbing gear is not required since there are no technical obstacles on this trail-less hike.

Recommended Maps

Zion National Park Topographic Map (ZNHA); see page 58.

Camping/Time Required

Experienced off-trail hikers may do this hike as a long day trip, but most do it as an overnight.

There are many sites suitable for camping along Right Fork. Campsites are found from the confluence with Left Fork upstream to "Double Falls." There are additional campsites along North Creek from the confluence downstream to the park boundary. Remember, campfires are not permitted.

Water Sources

North Creek is a reliable year round spring-fed stream. Small springs may be found along the canyon at the upper end of this hike. The water will need to be purified.

Season

Summer is the best time to hike Right Fork since the route requires crossing the shallow stream. Deerflies are sometimes a problem in early summer. Right Fork is known for its tremendous flash floods. Be sure to camp out of the flood plain if storms threaten.

Spring and fall are enjoyable times to make this hike as the west-draining canyon gets a fair amount of sunlight. From November through April the water can be quite chilly and there is a possibility of snow. Short excursions into the lower end of Right Fork can be rewarding almost anytime.

The Starting Point

The parking area used to access this hike is 6.9 miles (11.1 km) north of Virgin on the Kolob Terrace Road. Drive exactly .4 mile (.6 km) past the "Kolob Terrace Section" sign at the park boundary. Watch carefully for a small unimproved and unmarked dirt parking area tucked into the juniper forest on the right side of the road.

The Route

From the parking area, hike .2 mile (.3 km) southeast to the cliff rim overlooking North Creek. Walk east along the rim looking for a rock cairn which marks a rugged break in the cliffs and a steep Class II route descending down the lava-boulder-strewn slopes .2 mile (.3 km) to North Creek. You will need to scramble over boulders in places. A wrong turn will provide you with bushwhacking opportunities.

Follow North Creek upstream .5 mile (. 8 km) to the confluence of the Left and Right Forks. At the confluence proceed up Right Fork, initially along the south side of the creek where paths make the hiking easier. Eventually follow the easiest path along the stream bottom.

Trail Canyon is a wide opening to the south 1.3 miles (2.1 km) from the confluence. Notice the old corrals on each side of the creek prior to reaching another major side canyon entering from the south 1.2 miles (1.9 km) further. After another .3 mile (.5 km) a canyon enters from the north; about .6 mile (.9 km) farther pass another major side canyon entering from the south. Choose your own route along the canyon bottom through this area.

About .2 mile (.3 km) beyond, the canyon narrows at a nice pool. Continue 100 yards (90 m) to an interesting overhang where a side canyon enters from the north.

Follow the creekbed 1 mile (1.6 km) to "Double Falls," a beautiful set of waterfalls spilling into a spectacular blue-green pool. It is as restful and beautiful a spot as you will find in Zion National Park.

There is a high, brushy path around "Double Falls" on the south side of the creek. Watch for poison ivy in this area. From "Double Falls" to "Barrier Falls" the going gets more difficult as the route is strewn with large boulders which require scrambling to get around.

Continue another .5 mile (.8 km), past several inviting falls, cascades and pools before reaching "Barrier Falls" which marks the end of this hike by blocking upstream travel. The area has extensive riparian foliage. "Barrier Falls" appears to be a large mound of rock extending from the pool to the top of the waterfall above.

To return, retrace your route to the starting point.

Right Fork of North Creek—Distance Chart

	mi	km
(S) Parking area on Kolob Terrace Road	0	0
Break in lava cliffs	.2	.3
North Creek	.4	.6
Confluence of Left & Right Forks	.9	1.4
Trail Canyon	2.2	3.5
Overhang - canyon from north	5.5	8.9
"Double Falls"	6.5	10.5
"Barrier Falls"	7.0	11.3
(E) Parking area on Kolob Terrace Road	14.0	22.3

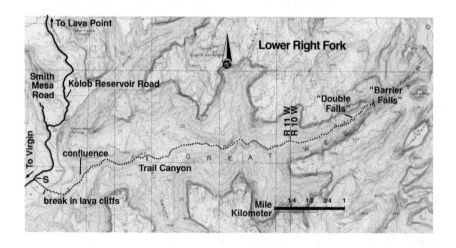

North Creek continues to cut a serpentine path through the sandstone bedrock.

NOTE: In order to reduce unacceptable impacts from unbridled use of this route, the National Park Service is proposing to limit the number of hikers. At the time of publication (11/96), no specific system has yet been established. Most likely, a permit will be required for both overnight and day use. Persons considering this route should contact a ranger or call (801) 772-3256 for updated information prior to initiating a hike.

Introduction/Difficulty

The Left Fork has gained popularity in recent years to the point where the nature of the hike is changing. Not long ago it was a seldom-visited wilderness canyon. As word of its beauty spread, it has perhaps gained too many admirers. Some have been careless, leaving behind litter, fire scars, altered and constructed campsites. The number of visitors has caused paths of use to appear along the canyon bottom. Please enjoy this special place gently. Avoid visiting on weekends or holidays if you can. Keep your group size small. If it is safe, camp where signs of your presence will be erased by the next high water.

There are two ways to visit the Left Fork—from the bottom or from the top. You may do this hike in reverse to gain access from the bottom or hike in from the lower Right Fork, see page 56. Our route comes in mid-way through Russell Gulch and passes a number of obstacles. Difficulties include: route finding through slickrock areas; swimming a deep, cold pool with gear; lowering yourself over several boulder obstacles with a rope; hiking or wading in water in a slippery, boulder-strewn stream bottom; and ascending a 400-foot (122 m) loose talus slope near the end of the hike. Despite its delicate beauty, the Left Fork is a challenging hike! Some narrow canyon areas in the center of this hike would be hazardous in a flood.

Equipment Needs

A 50-foot (15 m) length of climbing rope (many use 1" tubular webbing) will be needed at the boulder obstacles. Someone in your party should have rope management/descending experience. If you have doubts about downclimbing or body-rappelling, take rapelling gear for the obstacles.

Lightweight river bags or waterproof plastic trash sacks are useful for keeping essential gear dry. It is not worth it to lug along an air mattress for the one pool that you need to swim.

Wet suits may be needed on this hike during colder periods.

Recommended Maps

Zion National Park Topographic Map (ZNHA); see page 64.

Camping/Time Required

Some people hike this route in a long day, especially if they have done it before and know the way. Many have planned it as a day hike and ended up spending the night with little gear due to delays and missed turns along the way. Assess your canyoneering experience level; if there are any doubts, do it as an overnight trip.

Persons familiar with the hike usually require 7-10 hours to get through; others may take longer their first time on the route.

Overnight hikers must obtain a backcountry permit at one of the visitor centers. You don't need a permit for a day hike in this area, but it is prudent to inquire about current weather conditions before beginning your trip.

While there are some dry, but scenic, campsites located on the Northgate Peaks Trail and in Russell Gulch, most people camp from the "Subway" downstream where the canyon is wide and fresh water abundant.

Water Sources

The upper end of this hike is dry (and can be very hot.) When you reach Russell Gulch, stagnant potholes with water are often found. If you carry enough water you can reach the springs which supply the creek in Left Fork.

Season

Do this hike in mid-May or later, depending on snowfall accumulations and runoff at the higher elevations. The upper drainages of Left Fork (Russell Gulch, Blue Creek) should be flowing a trickle at most. The hike can usually be done until mid-October or so, except for periods of rainy weather or thunderstorms.

The Starting Point

The starting point for this hike is the well-signed Wildcat Canyon Trailhead located 16 miles north of Virgin, UT on the Kolob Terrace Road.

Since you end this hike at a different spot than you start, it is best to have two vehicles or arrange a shuttle.

The ending point is lower on the Kolob Terrace Road. From Virgin, UT drive north 8.1 miles (13.1 km) to the Left Fork Trailhead located on the east side of the road (1.7 miles, 2.7 km, north of the "Kolob

Terrace Section" boundary sign.) This dirt parking area is located in the pinyon-juniper forest and has room for about ten vehicles.

The Route

From Wildcat Canyon Trailhead hike east following the maintained trail 1.2 miles (1.9 km) to the Northgate Peaks junction. Hike south .1 mile (.2 km) on the Northgate Peaks Trail to the top of the hill where an obvious "path of use" leaves the trail on the left side heading southeast. Follow this path approximately 200 yards (183 m) and begin the descent into Russell Gulch on white sandstone.

Head down the slickrock to the southeast dropping approximately 200 feet (61 m) along a series of ledges to the southside of a drainage with ponderosa pine, aspen, and manzanita. Staying just to the right of the drainage, descend slickrock slopes to benchlands below, cross the drainage (usually dry), head east .2 mile (.3 km) to where you can see the bottom of Russell Gulch to the east. As you approach Russell Gulch, bear south before losing elevation, following intermittent paths .2 mile (.3 km) to a point between Russell Gulch and a tributary entering on your right. Work your way down a slickrock slope dropping 200 feet (61 m) to the crossing of Russell Gulch.

Continue south climbing 100 feet (30m) to a pink-colored slickrock saddle with a pair of hoodoos. Hike south-southeast down a slickrock bowl paralleling Russell Gulch, crossing two drainages that feed into Russell Gulch. As you approach a butte on the ridge south of this second drainage, hike in a southwest direction following hiker/game trails ascending the ridge top. Continue along this ridge with the Left Fork on your left and Russell Gulch on your right.

At this point you begin a steep, Class III, 200 vertical foot (61 m) descent into a cleft chute-route to a plunge pool in lower Russell Gulch near the confluence with Left Fork. Slowly and carefully make your way down this narrow sand and scree corridor, maintaining safe spacing with other hikers to avoid being hit with loose rock dislodged from above.

Proceed 60 yards (55 m) down Russell Gulch to the Left Fork confluence, .1 mile (.2 km) below the confluence. Work your way through a "boulder field" to a pour-off/plunge pool. There are three ways to negotiate this 12 foot (3.7 m) drop. 1. On the right side chimney down a crack between boulder and canyon wall, belay if necessary. Sometimes a log is found here to simplify this descent. 2. Set up belay and descend the boulder left of the crack. 3. Cross the left side of drainage working around a narrow exposed ledge to a small cave that leads directly into the plunge pool.

Continue downstream in the wash as the canyon narrows into a corridor. Immediately after a 90° right turn you will have to swim a 30 foot (9 m) pool followed immediately by a 15 foot (4.6 m) pool, which is also a swim. These pools are cold, especially during cooler months of the season.

Around the bend, a spring marks the beginning of the Left Fork creek. 100 yards (91 m) beyond, the stream cuts its way through a narrow gorge with overhanging ledges on either side. Some hardy souls stay in the cold creek bottom, which involves climbing over top chalkstone obstacles and swimming a 50 foot (15 m) long pool. The other option is to climb 10 feet (3 m) to a ledge system on the left side of the canyon. Follow the ledge with an overhang, which initially forces you to squat, waddle, crawl, and possibly hold your pack along this damp, slippery stretch. Continue along the ledge which opens up as you walk along the pools below. Follow the ledge into the vegetation above, then switch back down to a Class III slickrock descent to the canyon bottom. A stout ponderosa provides a good anchor from which to belay.

The next obstacle approximately .3 mile (.5 km) down canyon is Keyhole Falls, a 10 foot (3 m) drop. Loop your rope or webbing through the runner bolted to right side, or through the natural hole in sandstone on left side. Pool depth varies from flood to flood, but often it is waist deep or less.

Continue downstream around a right turn to a 10 foot (3 m) waterfall, which can be easily by-passed to the right on a ledge system. The canyon bends to the left where the stream disappears into a crack, cascading 15 feet (4.6 m) into inverted narrows known as the Subway. Stay to the left of the falls following a ledge system to where the canyon wall slopes more gradually to the canyon bottom. Double your rope or webbing through runners bolted in sandstone, lowering yourself to the stream below. This concludes the technical portion of this hike.

At this point you have come 5.1 miles (8.2 km) with 4.4 miles (7.1 km) to go. The route is simpler from here on, as major obstacles become fewer. There are spectacular cascades, nice pools and lots of boulders as the canyon opens up and becomes wider.

Two miles (3.2 km) below the Subway, as you approach the confluence with Little Creek, you will see a basaltic lava flow on your right. An abandoned trail climbs the south face of this lava flow into Lee Valley. Oftentimes hikers mistake this old trail for the exit to Left Fork Trailhead, a mistake that results in numerous overdue parties each year.

The next landmarks will be Little Creek and .25 mile (.4 km) beyond, you will cross Pine Springs Wash—both flow in from your right. From the Pine Springs Wash confluence, you can see the second basaltic lava flow on the right side of the canyon. This is where the route leaves the canyon for Left Fork Trailhead.

One-half mile (.8 km) down-canyon from Pine Springs Wash, the well cairned route up a steep pinyon-juniper covered talus slope leads to the plateau 400 feet (122 m) above where the basalt flow begins. From the top, follow the cairned route .8 mile (1.3 km) to the Left Fork Trailhead.

Left Fork of North Creek - Distance Chart

	mi	km
(S) Wildcat Canyon Trailhead	0	0
Northgate Peaks Trail Junction	1.2	1.9
Leave Northgate Peaks Trail	1.3	2.1
Russell Gulch crossing	2.6	4.2
Cleft-chute into Russell Gulch	3.7	6.0
Boulder/chimney obstacle	3.9	6.3
Cold swim pothole	4.3	6.9
"Keyhole Falls"	4.9	7.9
"The Subway"	5.1	8.2
Dinosaur tracks	6.9	11.1
Pine Springs Wash	7.8	12.6
Way out of the Left Fork	8.3	13.4
Top of basalt cliffs	8.7	14.0
(E) Parking Area on Kolob Terrace Road	9.5	15.3

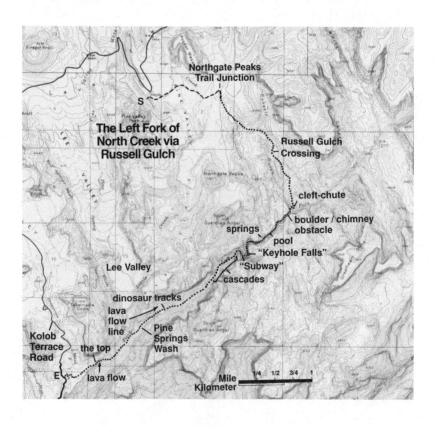

Zion is famous for its slot canyons--narrow chasms carved through sandstone by annual runoff.

Introduction/Difficulty

This route is regarded as one of the most adventurous and rugged backcountry hikes in the park. It travels through some of the most ecologically diverse and pristine areas in Zion.

Great West Canyon (not the Left Fork of North Creek as labeled on the 7.5′ USGS quad map) is the most difficult hike listed in this guide. Those hiking it should possess rappelling and rope management skills and be in top physical condition. Map reading and route finding skills are a must. Those going through the "Black Pool" should be excellent swimmers and prepared for cold water, even in the middle of summer. The pool temperature has been measured at 45° F (7° C) during mid-July.

Avoid this hike when thunderstorms threaten. The Right Fork drains a vast slickrock area which creates a raging river after rains.

Equipment Needs

A 120-foot (37 m) length of climbing rope, rappelling gear, and a few nylon runners will be needed at the obstacles. For those going through the "Black Pool," an air mattress is useful. Bug repellent is helpful if you camp during mosquito season or encounter deerflies.

Recommended Maps

Zion National Park Topographic Map (ZNHA); see page 71.

Camping/Time Required

Hikers should allow at least two full days (three is preferable) to complete this strenuous hike.

Good campsites exist near the "Wildcat Canyon Seeps," the potholes above the giant stairstep ledges, in the "Grand Alcove," and below "Double Falls" where the Right Fork Canyon widens.

Water Sources

Potholes may be sought out along the hike, but the quantity or quality of the water depends on recent rainfall. Some brackish seeping water is usually available at the "Wildcat Canyon Seeps."

Otherwise it is scarce until the "Grand Alcove," where springs feed the Right Fork of North Creek, which has a year round flow.

Season

The best times to make this hike are during late spring, summer or early fall. The first half of the hike can be quite hot during the warmest days of summer. Flash flooding makes the route impassable and dangerous.

The Starting Point

From Virgin drive to the West Rim Trailhead (just under Lava Point) via the Kolob Terrace Road. The route begins there. Hikers may wish to leave a vehicle at the Right Fork Parking Area (see page 57) where the hike ends.

The Route

As you begin the hike, follow the West Rim Trail about .1 mile (.2 km); at the junction make a right onto the Wildcat Canyon Trail, which soon leaves the plateau and drops until it reaches the usually-dry Blue Creek in Wildcat Canyon.

Leave the trail just before Blue Creek (backtrack if necessary) and follow the drainage. The cross-country route requires bushwhacking, log climbing, and boulder hopping. Proceed down Wildcat Canyon via any convenient route.

The canyon drops rather steeply until it is joined by a box canyon entering from the left. Continue down the dry drainage (often the walking will be easier on wildlife trails to the side of the streambed) to where a second canyon enters from the left (east) side. Prominent white cliffs surround you in all directions. Climb up to a low, sandy ridge to the right of the streambed and follow the crest parallel to Wildcat Canyon, approaching a third canyon entering from the left.

Drop down to cross the Wildcat drainage to the left (east) side, climb to a low saddle, and continue to the Left Fork of North Creek. Some brackish pothole seeps may be found by walking just south of point 6118 on the Zion topo map to where the drainage which flows from the southeast begins to drop into the Left Fork drainage. A large twin hoodoo on the hillside is a good landmark above the seeps. The largest potholes are toward the base of the seeps.

From the seeps, hike southeast, left of the drainage, up a gradual climb through meadows followed by groves of Gambel oak so thick you will have to circumvent them. Continue toward the crest at the southeast end of this verdant valley. Head to the left (east) of a small peak prominent on the crest; just south of the 6250 elevation line on the Zion topo. Pass through an oak forest carpeted with ferns.

The crest or saddle is the drainage divide between the Left and Right Forks of North Creek. There are dry campsites in this area. From the saddle you will experience breathtaking views of the Right Fork's eroded headwater drainage basin and Phantom Valley, recessed to the south.

Proceed around the east side of the small peak below 6250, dropping into a small drainage that parallels, but is west of, the northeast-most Right Fork drainage. There will be some steep spots; work your way around them, then along the drainage until it joins the Right Fork drainage. Continue about .1 mile (.2 km) then climb out of the drainage bottom to your right (west) before the canyon walls get too steep. If you come to an impassable dry waterfall, you have come too far; backtrack to escape the drainage bottom.

Once on the slopes to the west above the developing Right Fork Canyon, travel south, working up the slopes where convenient. Soon you must head upslope to gain the ridge; the climb can be a grind, especially if you choose a brushy route. There is a pretty hoodoo with a red top knot to the west.

Note the drainage developing at the base of the cliff to the west. Head southeast on the ridge (watch for paths) parallel to this drainage. After following the ridge about .5 mile (.8 km), notice that the west drainage becomes more open and brush free. This has been called the "giant staircase," as the normally dry drainage has periodic abrupt drops into potholes.

At this point it is much easier to walk in this dry west drainage until arriving at a point where the drainage drops steeply via a narrow fracture. Set up a belay if necessary. Descend the fracture about 10 yards (9 m), then traverse left and descend difficult Class III slickrock slopes down the ridge just left of the fracture. Set up a belay if necessary. The slickrock ridge leads to a steep, sandy wooded area; descend on a faint path adjacent to the drainage. After about 50 yards (45 m) enter a fissure. Turn right and leave the fissure before it drops through a small crack. Enter the original side drainage against the right hand cliffs, and follow it down some 20 yards (18 m). If there is a pool beneath the hanging drainage avoid it by veering left and following the ridge down to the slickrock ramp. Traverse right for about 30 yards (27 m) along the sloping ledge until you can make the short 3-yard (3 m) drop onto the floor of Right Fork Canyon.

Head down canyon. 55 yards (50 m) ahead you will encounter an obstacle—a huge boulder chockstone wedged between the canyon walls, requiring a scramble underneath the boulder where you climb immediately right onto a small shelf. Enter the pool (if present) on the extreme right to avoid swimming. You will get wet, but shouldn't have to swim if you hug this right wall.

About 30 yards (27 m) beyond is another huge rock which you can scramble underneath to the left. There is no use using the bolt in the wall on the right unless the tunnel is filled with debris.

68

Just beyond this obstacle the canyon makes an abrupt turn to the west. The canyon begins to narrow; .2 mile (.3 km) past the turn you will encounter an infamous obstacle, known as the "Black Pool," which varies from 25 yards (22 m) to over 100 yards (91 m) in length after a storm. To some hikers bypassing the "Black Pool" is the crux or most difficult part of this hike. Most people circumvent the pool by climbing left (south) just upstream from the pool, then traversing a series of easy ledges, and rappelling into the west end of the pool where they are past the deepest spots.

Another option is to pass the cold, deep, murky waters of the pool on an air mattress. Most folks do not choose this option due to the cold. A third option, if you have an expert climber in your party, is to do an exposed climb out on the right (north) side of the "Black Pool." This involves chimneying out of the narrows at the start of the "Black Pool," then making a move over to a tiny, slippery ledge on the right. The exposed climber must climb to a tree (look for slings on it) where he may set up a belay for those to follow. A fall is easily possible on this route—it is only advised for those with the skills and equipment to do it safely. From the tree you must traverse west above the pool. Look for runners and a bolt left by a previous party along this route. An exposed 5-foot (2 m) mantle move allows you to continue traversing. Finally you must get back into the stream bed where the first large drainage comes in from the right. This is done by downclimbing around the "corner," another awkward and exposed move.

Whichever route you choose, pass the "Black Pool" with utmost care. An accident in this area could easily be fatal.

About .2 mile (.3 km) downstream, another rappel over a waterfall can be avoided by climbing left and traversing 87 yards (80 m) to where a fracture permits you to descend to a ledge just two yards (2 m) above the streambed. Use a hand line or jump carefully to the canyon floor.

After hiking another .3 mile (.5 km) and doing considerable bouldering you will arrive at another dry fall which again is avoided by traversing around the left side of the canyon.

After completing .4 mile (.6 km) of scrambling over and around boulders, you will reach the upper end of the "Grand Alcove," which was named for its immense overhang. The alcove forms a beautiful amphitheater with hanging gardens and a sheltering overhang. As you approach, notice slowly-seeping stains on the north side of the canyon. Soon a crystal clear stream begins to drop through large potholes. This slippery streambed route may be straddled with care, but the potholes and cascades are very difficult to negotiate. Plan to get completely wet if you follow the streambed route.

Going to the west end of the ledge inside the amphitheater brings you to a cliff. Check the existing bolts; you may need to add a new runner to the anchor system. After proper testing, rappel to the shelf 12 yards (11 m) below. From this shelf, a short free rappel using a tree anchor will take you to the floor of the alcove.

About 100 yards (90 m) below the "Grand Alcove" we encounter the last major obstacle, "Barrier Falls," which acts as a barrier to hikers going upstream. After checking the bolt anchor system, carefully make the angled, slippery rappel adjacent to the falls.

Beyond this falls the canyon begins to widen as the stream cuts through the softer Kayenta formation. Start out on the right below the falls. You will have to pick your way past huge boulders with many pools and falls, and it is slow going. .5 mile (.8 km) below "Barrier Falls" you will reach "Double Falls." There is a trail around this drop, in the brush on the left (south) side of the canyon. There is a bit of poison ivy near the bottom.

We now follow the stream past cascades and small falls 5.6 miles (9 km) to the confluence of the Right and Left Forks. Refer to pages 57–58 for a more detailed description of this route.

From the confluence walk downstream on the right bank of North Creek, now augmented by the larger flow of the Left Fork, for 200 yards (185 m), then begin a long traverse to the right toward the cliff of lava caprock. Avoid the large areas of talus boulders. As you near the caprock, the climbing becomes milder and you will soon find a path of use traversing beneath the cliffs. After rounding a minor promontory, the path of use makes its way up through a Class II break in the cliffs. The road is just .2 mile (.3 km) to the northwest. If you miss the Right Fork Parking Area where you left your vehicle, be prepared to hike along the road a short way.

Right Fork of North Creek via Wildcat Canyon (Great West Canyon Route) — Distance Chart

	mi	km
(S) West Rim Trailhead	0	0
Wildcat-West Rim Trail Junction	.1	.2
Wildcat Canyon	1.7	2.7
Left-hand canyon I	2.4	3.9
Left-hand canyon II	3.9	6.3
Left-hand canyon III	4.8	7.7
Left Fork of North Creek	5.5	8.9
Pothole seeps	5.9	9.5
Saddle/divide	7.2	11.6
"Giant Staircase"	9.0	14.5
Floor of Right Fork	9.1	14.7
"Black Pool"	9.4	15.2
"Grand Alcove"	10.4	16.8
"Barrier Falls"	10.5	16.9
"Double Falls"	11.0	17.7
Confluence of Right & Left Forks	16.6	26.8
Top of lava cliffs	17.3	27.9
(E) Right Fork Parking Area	17.5	28.2

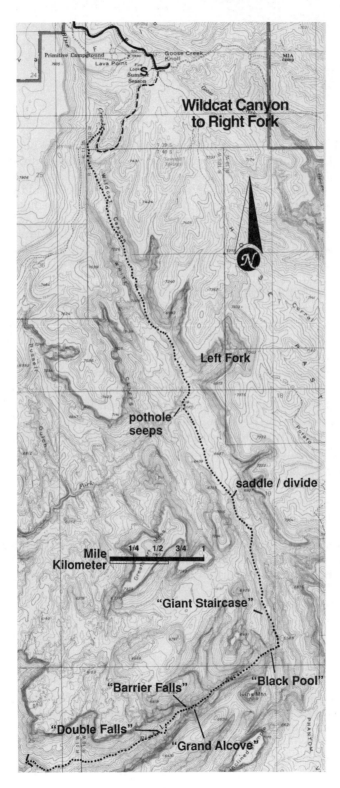

Wildcat Canyon to Right Fork

Left Fork

pothole seeps

saddle / divide

Mile
Kilometer

1/4 1/2 3/4 1

"Giant Staircase"

"Black Pool"

"Barrier Falls"

"Double Falls"

"Grand Alcove"

Introduction/Difficulty

This is one of the most difficult canyon hikes in this book.
Route finding in steep terrain is a major time consuming difficulty.
The route includes several obstacles such as steep Class III scree
slopes, a Class IV chimney, several waterfalls and deep, cold pools.
As there is no practical way to circumvent the pools, one must resort
to swimming distances as long as 25 yards (20 m) in chilly water.
Hikers need to be in excellent physical condition and be strong
swimmers—and should be adept at rock scrambling and cross-country route finding. Previous canyoneering experience is a must—a previous trip through the Zion Narrows should familiarize you with the
second half of this trip.

Hike this canyon when there are no water releases from Kolob
Reservoir. Water is usually released in late summer when irrigators
downstream from Zion need additional flow. Hiking the
streambed is only feasible during periods when the creek flow is
shut off or minimal. The Washington County Water Conservancy
District directs the water releases from Kolob Reservoir into Kolob
Creek. Before you begin your hike, it is your responsibility to veri-
fy flows by calling the District at their St. George, Utah, office.

Equipment Needs

Hikers should take 50 feet (15 m) of climbing rope or 1" tubular
webbing for belay use. Backpacks and gear should be waterproofed.
An air mattress might be useful for floating packs across the pools.
The best alternative is to use a wet suit to make the swims safer. **A
backcountry permit is needed for Kolob Creek and all tributary
canyons of the North Fork of the Virgin River.**

Recommended Maps

Zion National Park Topographic Map (ZNHA); see page 75.

Camping/Time Required

Level, above-flood campsites are scarce; wait until reaching the
North Fork of the Virgin River to set up camp. Most people do this
trip as an overnight hike.

Water Sources

A small stream is usually found in Kolob Creek where this route joins it. The creek may be dry downstream, but potholes hold standing water in all seasons. The Virgin River has a reliable flow year round. All water should be purified before drinking.

Season

This canyon is subject to flash flooding; obtain weather information with your permit at the Zion Canyon Visitor Center prior to the hike. Refer to pages 16–23 for information regarding the hazards of hiking the Zion Narrows.

Summer is the season to make this trip as the frigid water in the pools is at its warmest and the air temperature is warmer.

The Starting Point

From Virgin, UT, drive to the West Rim Trailhead (under Lava Point) via the Kolob Terrace Road. You must park here as a barricade blocks vehicle approaches to the park boundary.

The Route

Hike east down the dirt road 1.1 mile (1.8 km) to a "Y" in the road. Take the left road and continue less than .1 mile (.2 km) to another junction. (Note: These roads are not shown in true relation on the Zion topographic map.) Take a left and continue north .3 mile (.5 km) farther to a gate on the park boundary.

The next section of the approach is over private and BLM land. Continue 1.2 miles (1.9 km) to a major fork in the road. Take the right fork and continue .4 mile (.6 km) southbound, paralleling the canyon rim. You can see a major drop-off through the trees.

Work your way down through the trees to where you can see a precipitous vegetated way down off the rim. The slopes are very steep. You will be to the south of a ponderosa-covered stairstepped ridge ending with a small pinnacle. Head toward the southernmost drainage in this side canyon to avoid ledges where a belay will be mandatory. A vertical white sandstone wall rises to the south and southeast (your right).

Head down, generally following the small creekbed. Carefully work your way around the steep drop-offs, setting up a belay or hand line if you feel uncomfortable.

Continue to follow the drainage. It eventually begins to level out some—you are in a small canyon. There are drop-offs and small dry-falls, but you can work your way around them without too much trouble. The first major dryfall is about 20 feet (6 m) high. There is a rock bench above and to the left; climb up on this. You will now see a Class IV chimney that you can climb down to get to the wash below.

After bypassing some more boulders, you will reach the major obstacle in this side canyon—a 60 foot (18 m) dry fall. There is a huge "house size" alcove about 10 yards (9 m) upstream. Climb up the slope opposite the alcove (to the right of the drainage) following a faint path of use. When you crest the small brushy ridge follow the path below a large ponderosa pine at about the same elevation; then continue toward a second one just barely in view (it has a fire scar near its base). Take care on these steep brushy slopes. Continue just past the second ponderosa and begin working your way down the steep slope. Stay near the trees—although it seems unlikely, you can work your way down this steep slope to the wash bottom. If you have misgivings, have one person drop their pack and scout out the route. Use a belay if anyone in your party is nervous.

Continue down the drainage, working around the small dryfalls. There are two final falls that prevent easy access to Kolob Creek. Go left to bypass both. Traverse left at the second dryfall until you can see the Kolob Creek bottom.

Kolob Creek usually has water flowing in it at this point, although it often dries up before reaching the Virgin River.

You can take an interesting side trip up Kolob Creek Canyon, a narrow and picturesque gorge with high vertical walls. There is a 5 yard (5 m) waterfall with a deep pool at the base of the falls on Kolob Creek just above the mouth of Oak Creek. The Oak Creek tributary drops off about 16 yards (15 m) into Kolob Creek precluding travel up Oak Creek.

Starting down Kolob Creek, you will pass a small dry drainage coming in from the left. The canyon soon swings to the right and shortly takes more jogs to the right and left. About .7 mile (1.1 km) after entering Kolob Creek you arrive at a ledge dropping about 8 feet (2 m) into a 10 yard (9 m) long pool. It's time to swim! Just .1 mile (.2 km) beyond, the canyon narrows with sheer walls on both sides. You can see southeast down canyon a good distance. A bit downstream you reach two ponds adjacent to each other. The exact number of pools, and their depth, varies with how much water has recently been in the canyon. You are passing through a corner of the Deep Creek Wilderness Study Area (BLM) for about .5 mile (.8 km) before entering Zion National Park. All boundaries are unmarked.

Following the canyon you soon encounter the largest pool along the trek. The waterfall is 20 feet (6 m) high, dropping into a cold, deep pool about 22 yards (20 m) long. There is a bolt on the boulder from which you may rappel (after checking the bolt) into the pool. However, it is easier to climb going down the right side with a helping hand from a fellow hiker. Then the jump is less than 10 feet (3 m). It's a jump you'll always remember—ICY!

Continuing down canyon, the streambed weaves back and forth and small pools are often present. If you're lucky, most will be dry. There are some beautiful narrows along Kolob Creek. Continue to boulder hop downstream. After a final few bends you arrive at the Virgin River. There is a small campsite just to the right. For the remainder of this hike, refer to the Zion Narrows via the North Fork, page 16.

Kolob Creek -Distance Chart

	mi	km
(S) West Rim Trailhead	0	0
"Y" in dirt road	1.1	1.8
Second "Y"	1.2	1.9
Park boundary gate	1.5	2.4
Lower Road Fork	2.7	4.4
Leave rim dirt road	3.1	5.0
Arrive at Kolob Creek	4.0	6.5
First major pool	4.7	7.6
Sheer walls	4.8	7.7
Largest Kolob Creek pool (icy)	5.3	8.5
Kolob Creek/North Fork confluence	8.0	12.9
(E) Temple of Sinawava	14.8	23.9

Mileages on this hike are deceiving. It often takes four hours to travel one mile in upper Kolob Creek Canyon.

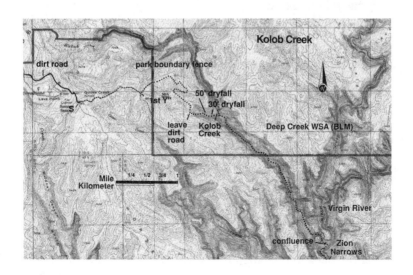

Introduction/Difficulty

Deep Creek and the North Fork are major tributaries of the Virgin River, but Deep Creek generally carries more and clearer water. Deep Creek passes through basaltic lava flows, and footing is more difficult and slippery over the volcanic boulders. There is extensive bushwhacking on this route. Hikers are advised to hike the Narrows via the North Fork prior to taking the Deep Creek route. Access is longer and more difficult to get into Deep Creek.

Equipment Needs

See page 16 for information on equipment needed while hiking the Zion Narrows.

Recommended Maps

Webster Flat, UT (USGS 7.5′ quad); see page 80.
Cogswell Point, UT (USGS 7.5′ quad); see page 81.
Temple of Sinawava, UT (USGS 7.5′ quad); see page 81.

Camping/Time Required

Those planning to hike Deep Creek and the narrows should allow three days or more if the weather is stable. While the mileage is not great, the going is slow.

Numerous locations have been used as campsites along Fife Creek and Deep Creek, particularly at the Fife/Deep Creek and O'Neil/Deep Creek confluences. Below O'Neil Creek, one can find campsites scattered along the entire route.

Water Sources

Stream water is located all along this hike; it must be purified before drinking.

Season

Much of this hike involves wading; therefore summer is the time to do it. Refer to the information beginning page 16 for information regarding hiking in the Zion Narrows. The threat of flash flood is as imminent in Deep Creek as elsewhere in the Narrows. Deep Creek takes more days to hike than the North Fork, therefore the long range weather forecast is more important. Meteorologists can predict the weather no more than a day or two in advance with any certainty.

The Starting Point

From the intersection of Center and Main in downtown Cedar City turn east on Center Street. St. Rt. 14 heads east taking you past Right-Hand Canyon, the impressive chasms near Ashdown Gorge, and the gentle aspen-covered slopes around Woods Ranch. Continue past the USFS Cedar Canyon Campground and drive under the pink cliffs to the "sandcuts." Turn right on the Webster Flat Road, Dixie National Forest Route 052, 14.7 miles (23.7 km) from Cedar City. The road is unpaved, but most passenger type vehicles can travel it without difficulty in good weather conditions. Continue past Webster Flat, the USFS Deer Haven Group Campground, and the signed Dixie National Forest boundary where you leave national forest land. Now the road loses elevation as it takes you past several side roads. Continue until you reach a flat scenic valley with a small creek meandering through. You have arrived at Fife Creek, and the hike begins at the culvert. Lava boulders and aspen are found to either side of the creek, as it exits the meadow valley.

The Route

Deep Creek Route - Starting Point Mileage Chart

	mi	km
Center & Main, Cedar City	0	0
Webster Flat Road	14.8	23.9
Deer Haven Group Campground	16.9	27.3
Dixie National Forest Boundary	18.8	30.3
Fife Creek, meadow (S)	21.0	33.9

From the Fife Creek culvert, begin the hike by walking down the path to the left of the creek, which will sometimes be dry at this point. You will need to climb two fences during this first part of the hike. Be careful not to break them down. After .3 mile (.5 km) you will pass a gentle valley entering from the left.

Just downstream cross a log "worm" fence on the right side of the valley. Stay on the right side of the creek. Near a lava rock outcrop about 75 yards (68 m) downstream from the fence you will notice a small drainage coming into Fife Creek from the right (west). Go up this drainage, away from Fife Creek, then pick up a path to the southwest which continues uphill where it connects with an abandoned dirt road. The road descends slowly into the valley, soon taking you to Big Spring, a rushing torrent and the main source of Fife Creek.

Follow the old road past the spring. Soon the abandoned road nears the creek then climbs and traverses the western side of the canyon as the stream drops sharply. About .4 mile (.7 km) beyond where the road leaves the streambed just below Big Spring, an unmarked path leaves the road at the left. Our route follows this path.

Now the path assumes a wilderness quality as it continues to descend the west side of the canyon and gives you several views of photogenic cascades and small waterfalls in the stream below. You will cross a fence as you arrive at the Deep/Fife Creek confluence. A nice campsite is located a short distance upstream on the west bank of Deep Creek through the thick brush.

From the confluence, the route now traverses down the west (right) bank of Deep Creek high above the stream and past impressive lava cliffs on the opposite wall. Soon the path drops down to the stream where several campsites are located at the O'Neil Gulch (West Fork)/Deep Creek confluence.

Beyond O'Neil Gulch, the terrain and vegetation change considerably. Instead of lush fir forest, the predominant tree is now Gambel oak. Rolling hills replace the sandstone and lava ledges which earlier formed deep canyons. Downstream from O'Neil Gulch a rough stock trail climbs immediately to a bench on the right bank. Note that the slopes west of the creek are Gambel oak covered, while the east slopes support fir and pine. This path continues on the bench through the oak for 1.2 mi (1.9 km) often disappearing in the brush, but it soon returns to the stream. From now on it will be difficult to hike with dry boots. Continue downstream, staying near the stream for 1.5 miles (2.4 km), to where benches become lower and easier to cross, although they are increasingly more brush covered as you near Corral Canyon.

The route continues downstream past a volcanic outcrop on the right, just .3 mile (.5 km) above Crystal Creek. After Crystal Creek,you will pass under several lava cliffs and finally the stream begins cutting its way through the top of the Navajo Sandstone; the beginning of the Deep Creek Narrows. This is BLM-administered land, the Deep Creek Wilderness Study Area.

The sheer sandstone walls rise rapidly as the creek cuts deeper into the Navajo. There are several good campsites which offer some protection in the event of a flash flood. The walking is often difficult and slippery along the boulder-strewn banks and in the stream. Several deep pools can be avoided. The Zion National Park boundary is unmarked.

Progress is slow in the spectacular Deep Creek Narrows, but you will eventually arrive at the Deep Creek/North Fork confluence. The route follows the North Fork of the Virgin River, now augmented by both tributaries. Refer to page 16 for information on the remainder of this hike.

Deep Creek—Distance Chart

	mi	*km*
(S) Fife Creek Culvert	0	0
Dry drainage/gentle valley	.3	.5
Big Spring	.8	1.3
Leave old road	1.3	2.1
Fife Creek/Deep Creek confluence	2.2	3.5
Deep Creek/O'Neil Gulch (West Fork) confluence	3.9	6.3
Corral Canyon	7.2	11.6
Crystal Creek	8.6	13.9
Deep Creek/North Fork confluence	14.9	24.0
(E) Temple of Sinawava	22.6	36.5

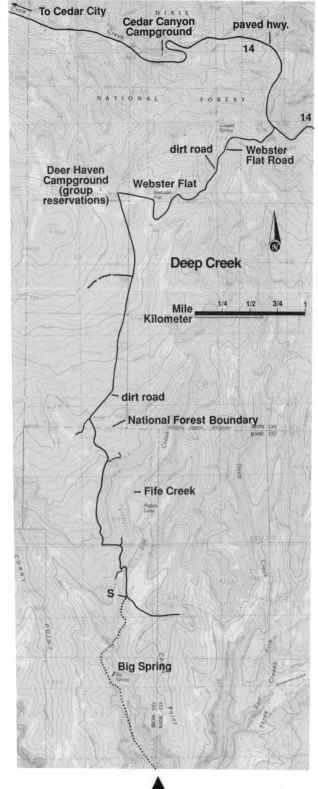

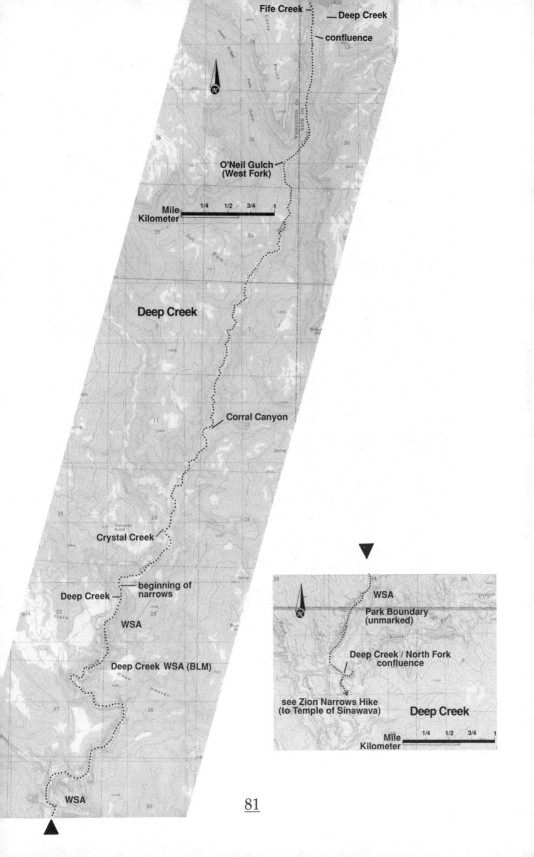

Fife Creek

— Deep Creek

— confluence

O'Neil Gulch
(West Fork)

Mile
Kilometer

1/4 1/2 3/4 1

Deep Creek

Corral Canyon

Crystal Creek

beginning of
narrows

Deep Creek —

WSA

Deep Creek WSA (BLM)

WSA

WSA

Park Boundary
(unmarked)

Deep Creek / North Fork
confluence

see Zion Narrows Hike
(to Temple of Sinawava)

Deep Creek

Mile
Kilometer

1/4 1/2 3/4 1

West Fork, Taylor Creek

The Finger Canyons of the Kolob exhibit some of the finest scenery on Earth. The massive stone cliffs, colored a brilliant red, form cathedral-like vistas on the grandest scale. Most visitors to Zion never see the Kolob Canyons, even though they are easily accessed from the Kolob Canyons Exit #40 off I-15, 17 miles (27 km) south of Cedar City and 39 miles (63 km) from Zion Canyon.

It takes about one hour to drive from Zion Canyon to the Kolob Canyons. A visitor center was constructed just off the freeway in 1984 by the Zion Natural History Association and donated to the National Park Service. Park personnel are available to answer questions, sell maps and publications, and issue backcountry permits.

Introduction/Difficulty

The North Fork of Taylor Creek is a short hike. A few rotten stumps, relics of pioneer logging activity, remind the hiker that this area was not added to Zion National Park until 1937. The footing is more difficult than the Middle or South Forks due to an abundance of volcanic boulders which have tumbled down from Horse Ranch Mountain. The volcanics are more slippery than other rock of the area.

Equipment Needs

No special equipment is needed on this hike.

Recommended Maps

Zion National Park Topographic Map (ZNHA); see page 86.

Camping/Time Required

This hike can be done in one-half day. While the Middle and South Forks of Taylor Creek are closed to camping, it is permitted in this area. Permits are limited in this area. Inquire at the Kolob Canyons Visitor Center for more information.

Water Sources

The Middle Fork of Taylor Creek and the lower portion of the North Fork carry water year round.

Season

The North Fork can be hiked whenever the general area is snow free, runoff is minimal, and there are no thunderstorms predicted.

Snow slides off the cliffs at the upper end of the canyon, creating drifts that last into May or even June. When this snow is deep and hard it is possible to walk over some boulder obstacles. Use caution moving about on these snow accumulations.

Vegetation green-up usually occurs here in May; fall colors peak in October. Thundershowers can alter the nature of the canyon bottom.

The Starting Point

Drive 2 miles (3.2 km) east of the Kolob Canyons Visitor Center to the Taylor Creek Trailhead, where the trail up the Middle Fork begins. You will initially follow this trail.

The Route

Take the Taylor Creek Trail (which goes up Middle Fork) to the North Fork/Middle Fork confluence. The Larsen cabin, built in 1929, is located just west of the confluence of the Middle and North Forks of Taylor Creek.

From the confluence, the route follows the North Fork, which enters from the left. The streambed will carry a slight flow and is your main source of drinking water in this area.

After you pass the first left-hand canyon, which drains the area just west of Horse Ranch Mountain, the streambed will turn east and be strewn with lava boulders, making the footing more uneven. You soon arrive at the second left-hand canyon. Scramble over a few large boulders and deadfalls, pass the third left-hand canyon, and walk by a prominent monolith on the left. Look up at the spectacular—even for Zion—vertical wall to the south.

Beyond this point the hiking becomes much rougher. When you arrive at a sheer precipice on the right you must bypass several obstacles during the next 300 yards (274 m). Now the banks of the streambed are quite flat, and there are a couple of potential camp-sites.

Continuing up the narrowing canyon, you soon arrive at a 20 foot (6 m) high dry fall which will stop the progress of most hikers. It may be bypassed by backtracking 45 yards (41 m) and climbing a Class III slope on the north side. Within the next 160 yards (146 m) two more obstacles appear: the first is passable, but the second will stop all except technical climbers.

North Fork of Taylor Creek - Distance Chart

	mi	km
(S) Taylor Creek Trailhead	0	0
Middle/North Fork confluence	1.2	1.9
First left-hand canyon	1.7	2.7
Second left-hand canyon	1.9	3.1
Third left-hand canyon	2.2	3.6
20-ft dry fall	3.0	4.9
(E) Taylor Creek Trailhead	6.0	9.8

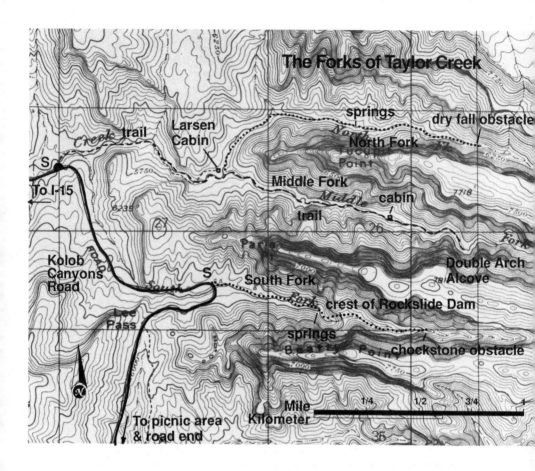

The Forks of Taylor Creek

Creek trail

Larsen Cabin

springs

North Fork

dry fall obstacle

Middle Fork

cabin

trail

S

To I-15

Kolob Canyons Road

Paria

Lee Pass

S

South Fork

Double Arch Alcove

crest of Rockslide Dam

springs

chockstone obstacle

To picnic area & road end

Mile
Kilometer

1/4   1/2   3/4   1

12 THE SOUTH FORK OF TAYLOR CREEK

Introduction/Difficulty

The spectacular South Fork of Taylor Creek can be explored by hiking through easy cross-country terrain in several hours. A steep hike up a 245-foot (75 m) high sandy slope covered with scrub oak presents the only difficulty.

Equipment Needs

No special equipment is needed on this hike.

Recommended Maps

Zion National Park Topographic Map (ZNHA); see page 86.

Camping/Time Required

The South Fork is closed to overnight camping; the Park Service considers this a day use area because of its close proximity to the road.

Water Sources

There is fresh water at the base of the massive rock slide 645 yards (590 m) from the road, but water is not usually found upstream.

Season

The hike can be safely completed any time the area is not snow or ice covered. The upper end of the canyon is likely to have considerable snow into May, but it does not present a hiking difficulty.

The Starting Point

Drive 3.1 miles (5 km) east of the Kolob Canyons Visitor Center. The paved road makes a sweeping hairpin curve as it enters and leaves the South Fork Canyon. The route begins at the north end of the parking area on the outside of the turn.

The Route

Walk down into the canyon from the left side of the parking area (north side of the curve) via a sloping open path. After about 100 yards (90 m) you will approach the canyon bottom; near there you will pick up a well-worn unofficial trail. From here the path traverses up the canyon, paralleling the stream for about 450 yards (411 m) and avoiding the thick willows growing in the bottom.

As you arrive at a section of wall on your right with some pretty black stains, there will be spring seepage in the canyon bottom in the driest season.

Several routes cross over the large rock slide (the surface rocks have degraded to sandy soils) now looming in the east. The easiest route follows the rounded scree ridge on the left (north) side of the canyon. As you start up and leave the small side wash, you will hike up a 30-foot (9 m) high dirt ridge. Go left when you reach the crest. Watch for paths through the Gambel oak. Cross the rock slide at its low point on the left (north) side of the canyon.

Beyond the crest lies a small pond (often dry) with cattails and stagnant water. This pond is the remnant of "Beatty Lake," which geologists believe was formed when the huge rock slide blocked and dammed this canyon.

After leaving the pond, hike through a large flat forested area; sediment deposited by the stream after the slide occurred. Notice the multiple changing stream channels, a sign of continuing stream activity behind the rock slide dam.

Continue up the verdant flat region behind the rockslide. The most open way is on the right (south) side of the canyon where the active wash has somewhat cleared the path. After .5 mile (.8 km) the canyon will narrow.

As you continue, the canyon becomes more narrow and begins to climb. During the winter months the walls in this area funnel enormous avalanches of snow into the bottom of the canyon. Often the snow remains well into May. This area provides some good shade in summer.

Our route ends at the first obstacle, a huge chockstone boulder. Although it may be bypassed to the left, more difficult obstacles will be encountered immediately beyond. Active erosional processes make the head of this canyon subject to rapid and severe change.

South Fork of Taylor Creek—Distance Chart

	mi	km
(S) Hairpin Curve Parking Area	0	0
Downstream end of rock slide dam/ seepage area	.4	.6
Rock slide crest	.7	1.2
Chockstone obstacle	1.6	2.6
(E) Hairpin Curve Parking Area	3.2	5.2

Top left : Claret Cup Cactus
Top right : Ringtail
Bottom : Coachwhip snake
(non-poisonous)

GLOSSARY

Anchor: Natural or artificial protrusions (such as trees, boulders, pitons or bolts) solidly and securely fixed, so that a climbing rope cannot pull or jerk the anchor loose, even if the climber falls.

Belay: To secure another hiker or climber against a possible fall— usually using a rope and one's own body, a natural anchor, or man-made hardware of various types.

BLM: Bureau of Land Management, a sister agency of the National Park Service in the Department of the Interior. The BLM administers millions of acres of undeveloped lands in Utah under multiple use principles. Under Congressional mandate prime areas are being studied as potential additions to the Wilderness System, including 12 areas adjacent to Zion National Park.

Cairn: Rocks stacked into a pile which is obviously manmade and stands out from the surrounding terrain. Cairns have sometimes been used to mark cross-country routes. Small cairns consisting of two or three rocks stacked vertically are often referred to as "ducks." Hikers should not build new cairns within the park, as backcountry ethics discourage "works of man" in wild areas.

Chimney: Used in climbing to describe a narrow chute or crack wide enough for the body. Climbing a chimney is accomplished by using the whole body, arms and legs in opposing "scissor-like" moves against both walls. Chimneys are usually difficult to protect.

Chockstone: A boulder or rock wedged between the opposite sides of a crack or narrow canyon. An artificial chock is a climbing device often made of aluminum; when jammed properly into a crack it provides a secure anchor.

Classes of Climbing Difficulty*

> Class I Easy walking, but more difficult than on maintained trails.
> Class II Difficult walking where hands must be used occasionally for balance or for handholds. Sturdy boots are necessary.
> Class III Handholds and footholds are necessary. The exposure or difficulty is such that some may wish a belay.
> Class IV All climbers should use a belay. Climbing hardware may be necessary to anchor belays. A fall in this terrain would have serious consequences.
> Class V The most difficult climbing possible without depending on manmade aids.
>
> *Such a classification tends to be subjective, since what may be Class III to one person may be Class IV to another, but provides a rough guide to climbers.

Couloir: A natural break or corridor in cliffs, often caused by fractures or faults.

Dryfall: "A waterfall without water" one desert hiker calls this feature. Dryfalls are usually vertical drops in dry drainages that form waterfalls during flood or snowmelt runoff. Often rubbed smooth from debris action, they are almost always difficult to get around. Sometimes called "pour offs."

Friction: To climb steep areas where the absence of protrusions make it necessary to rely on the friction of hands and feet on the rock. Climbing on smooth rock can be dangerous if belays are not possible.

Hanging Drainage (or Hanging Canyon): A side canyon whose mouth lies above the floor of the main canyon it drains into. Often difficult to access, their rate of erosion lags behind that of the main canyon because they drain a smaller watershed.

Handline: A securely-anchored rope often used as a help to climbers moving up or down steep slopes. Used in situations where the drop is short or fall danger minor. Rappel techniques or a belay should be used when in doubt.

Hoodoo: A remnant rock pillar or pedestal, often capped with harder rock, where the softer surrounding rock has been eroded away. The outcrop is often found in crazy, interesting, or unusual shapes in slickrock country.

Mantle: A climbing move where hands are placed, palms down, on a chest-high or higher ledge or protrusion on the rock. With a fluid movement the body springs and is lifted by pushing up and extending the arms. A foot is then lifted over the ledge.

Narrows: A term used in the Colorado Plateau country to describe a drainage where erosion has cut a small-in-width canyon with relatively high vertical relief. Narrows come in all shapes and sizes, are often a destination for hikers and are almost always beautiful.

Path of Use: A path which has been worn along cross-country routes by hikers or wildlife, but is not a maintained trail.

Pothole: Holes which are common in sandstone drainage bottoms, especially in intermittent streams. Potholes are usually found at the base of small waterfalls and cascades; they are caused by the abrasive action of water and debris and the inherent cementation weakness of the rock (especially wet sandstone). Varying in size, shape, and depth, some potholes hold water through dry summer periods.

Protection: The manner or devices used to guard against falls or injury; usually by a rope secured by anchors (natural or manmade) and attached to the climber.

Rappel: To descend a slope or cliff by sliding down a climbing rope. Although potentially a safe maneuver, rappelling accidents are the most common rock climbing/mountaineering accident. A person wishing to rappel must know how to set up and use a reliable system, from anchors to the brake-descending system used on the rope.

Rockfall: A continuous, daily occurrence in canyon country where rock and debris travel down vertical or steep slopes. Rockfalls can be a single rock or thousands of tons. Hikers should avoid areas where fresh rock has fallen or sand is coming down. These areas are likely to experience more rockfall as disturbed pieces break loose.

Route: A recommended direction of cross terrain travel. Routes may follow paths made by wildlife, other hikers, or drainages. In other cases, the route may be indistinguishable across slickrock or through brushy areas.

Runner: Usually a loop of tubular nylon webbing tied with a water knot. Used extensively in rappelling. Often left behind with a rappel ring.

Saddle: The lowest point on a ridge. The "pass" between two higher hills, buttes, or peaks.

Scramble: To climb over small ledges, rocks and obstacles without the use of technical climbing equipment. Handholds are usually required.

Scree: Loose sand, gravel and rocks on steep slopes which may move when stepped upon. Scree can be dangerous on steeper slopes which lead to drop offs or if rockfall is a hazard.

Slickrock: Bare, smooth rock which may be either flat or sloping, in multiple shapes and colors. On the Colorado Plateau slickrock usually refers to extensive exposed sandstone areas.

Talus: A pile of rocks or boulders at the base of a cliff or caught on a hillside. Similar to scree slopes.

RECOMMENDED READING

(All references are available through the Zion Nat. Hist. Assn.)

Books

Zion the Trails

Revised 1996, spiral bound pocket guide to Zion National Park's most popular trails. Compiled by Bob Lineback and Published by ZNHA.

Exploring Southern Utah's Land of Color

Abbreviated history of the Indians, settlements and ghost towns in Southern Utah. By A. F. Bruhn.

Introduction to Geology, Zion National Park

Informative and easy to comprehend description of how unique and varied formations make up Zion. By A. Warneke.

Kolob Canyon, Zion National Park

Colorful and descriptive information on the Northwest area of Zion. By A. Leach.

Zion, Towers of Stone

Excellent work that summarizes the essence of Zion, its landscape, plants, animals, and people. By J. L. Crawford. Also available in German and French.

Maps (A must!)

Zion Topo

Zion Topo, coated

For mail orders only 1-800-635-3959

For information
about Zion National Park 1-801-772-3256